W9-ASL-525

THE ESPRESSO ENCYCLOPEDIA

The Complete Guide
For The Home Preparation
Of European Café-Quality
Espresso, Cappuccino & Caffè Latte

Bernard N. Mariano and Jill West

Published by:
Trendex International, Inc.
1540 Merchandise Mart
Chicago, IL 60654

Copyright© 1994 Bernard N. Mariano and Jill West

Cover design: Mel Winer
Contributing Editor: Ruth L. West

All rights reserved. No portion of this book may be reproduced
by any means without permission in writing from the publisher.
Requests for permission to make copies of any part of this work
should be mailed to:

TRENDEX INTERNATIONAL, INC.
1540 Merchandise Mart, Chicago, IL 60654

Library of Congress Catalog No.: 94-9014C
ISBN   0-9643222-1-8

Second Edition
Printed in the United States of America

ACKNOWLEDGMENTS

Coffee is an expression of friendship and hospitality throughout the world, and the Specialty Coffee Industry is a remarkably hospitable business. The authors wish to express their thanks to everyone devoted to the Specialty Coffee Industry; retailers, roasters, sales representatives, manufacturers, importers, trade associations, journalists, and, of course, the consumer, all of whom have made our experience in this industry a very rewarding challenge.

With special thanks to Ruth West for her invaluable support of every Trendex program.

Table of Contents

Chapter 4: Systems, Controls and Switches

Chapter 6: Preparing Espresso at Home

Chapter 7: Frothing and Steaming Milk

Chapter 8: Recipes

Chapter 9: Care and Maintenance

Chapter 10: Help, Support & Resources

Chapter 11: The Espresso Encyclopedia

Chapter 12: Buyer's Guide to Equipment

Appendix:

IMPORTANT NOTICE

The information in this book is not intended to supersede the information contained in the instruction manuals supplied by manufacturers of espresso and cappuccino equipment.

Since each machine has its own operating specifications and safety features, the authors and publisher disclaim all liability incurred in connection with the generalized information contained in this book.

Please carefully read the operational instructions and safety notices supplied with your machine.

ABOUT THIS BOOK

The Espresso Encyclopedia is designed for all espresso enthusiasts, from the novice considering the purchase of a new machine, to connoisseurs interested in fine-tuning their espresso techniques. It is our hope that this book will help you extract optimum performance from your machine, and help you protect your investment through proper care and maintenance of your equipment.

American consumers are maturing, not only in their appreciation of espresso-related beverages but also in their choice of more sophisticated home equipment. More and more machines are available on the market, at a wide range of retail price points. In most cases the old adage holds true, "you get what you pay for" with espresso equipment. We hope this book will help you understand why prices vary and help you make an informed decision to match machine features to your personal needs.

Although the process of preparing espresso and espresso-related beverages on the surface seems relatively simple, it is a complex endeavor that requires a reasonable amount of knowledge and a great deal of practice. Learning to extract café-quality espresso from your machine is like learning to ride a bicycle. It takes practice, but, once you gain the skills, looking back, it all seems so simple.

We have chosen not to make brand recommendations. Instead, we have provided a general overview of all types of equipment readily available, and we ask that you rely on your specialty retailer to assist you in your purchase of the right equipment for your home use.

You do not need to become an espresso machine engineer, but with a general understanding of what is happening inside an espresso machine, along with some basic rules, you will easily develop the skills to thoroughly enjoy the delightful taste and pleasure in preparing any number of espresso-related beverages in the comfort of your own home.

WHAT IS ESPRESSO?

Espresso is a method of quickly extracting the heart of the coffee flavor under pressure in single servings. Some believe the origin of the word is from the French "exprès" (especially for you), which may explain the common misspelling of espresso with an "x". Others cite the Italian "espresso", for rapid or fast, as the source.

Since Italians hold the lead in the manufacture of equipment and daily consumption, they are considered the innovators of what we now know as espresso.

True espresso is a complex beverage, combining a special blend of arabica beans, darkly roasted, finely ground, densely packed and quickly brewed under pressure in individual servings. Properly brewed espresso with crema has a uniquely smooth and creamy, bittersweet flavor that captures the full essence of the beans, a distinctive flavor not found in any other type of coffee.

WHAT IS CREMA?

CREMA ("schiuma" in Italian) is the heart and soul of true espresso flavor. Crema is the foamy, golden brown extraction that develops in the filter holder and encrusts the top of your espresso serving.

Delicate oils in the espresso grind form colloids, very fine suspended gelatin-like particles with a very slow rate of sedimentation. Overextracted espresso releases bitter oils that break down the colloids and dissipate the crema.

Crema is evidence that the right amount of fresh coffee was ground to the proper consistency, and a precise amount of water at the correct temperature was quickly forced under pressure through the fine espresso grind.

Unfortunately, crema is not easy to achieve. But learning all the secrets to consistently brewing espresso with crema at home makes the reward well worth the effort.

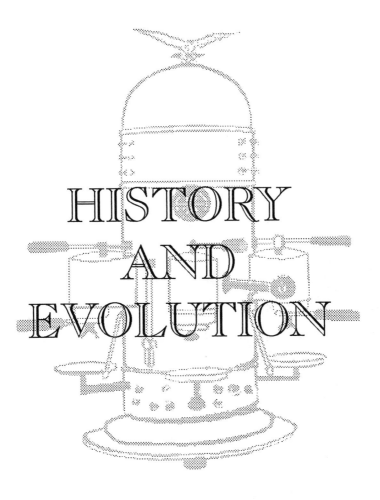

HISTORY
AND
EVOLUTION

HISTORY OF ESPRESSO IN NORTH AMERICA

It all began with the wave of immigrants to the United States from central and southern Italy in the early 1900's. Many of these Italians brought their Neopolitan coffee makers and settled in ethnic enclaves in cities like New York, Boston, Chicago, San Francisco and Toronto, where they continued to enjoy their pungent coffee. This special brew was often referred to as "Italian" coffee.

In fact, the coffee brewed in the Neopolitan-type coffee maker was not espresso as we know it today. But these immigrants clung to their old world ritual, enjoying their "Italian" coffee for breakfast, after lunch and dinner. Many first- and second-generation Italian families still favor their Neopolitan pots.

During the 1930's, many Italians traded their beloved Neopolitans for the newly developed Moka, invented in Italy by Alfonso Bialetti in 1933. Although still not producing what we know as espresso today, the stove-top Moka provided a small amount of pressure to extract more of the rich coffee flavor.

One major factor in popularizing espresso in North America was the popularity of Italian restaurants, where espresso is considered an absolute necessity by Italian patrons as an after-lunch or after-dinner beverage.

Another contributing factor during the 1960's and '70's was the number of North Americans who visited Europe, specifically Italy, where they were introduced to the wonderful taste sensations of espresso, cappuccino and caffè latte.

In most of Europe, cappuccino and caffè latte are considered breakfast drinks, rarely consumed past noon. But Americans embrace their milk-based espresso concoctions around-the-clock, probably because most are not really accustomed to the deep and penetrating bittersweet flavor of true espresso. Espresso is an acquired taste, and, when brewed properly, a crema espresso can convert a drip coffee drinker for life.

Europeans do not understand the American trend toward masking what they consider to be the true espresso flavor with milk and flavorings. If you order just a "latte" in Italy, you will be served a glass of cold milk. But more than 80% of the espresso beverages served in North America are milk-based. Although espresso-related beverages account for only 2% of total coffee consumption in North America, the percentage is growing very rapidly.

This popularity has reached such a peak that today there are espresso machines located in fast food restaurants and convenience stores. You will find espresso machines in many department stores, book stores, beauty salons, apparel stores, and, in the Northwest, even dentist's offices and service stations serve espresso. During the past 15 years, we have seen a virtual explosion of even more espresso bars and coffeehouses nationwide that has turned espresso, cappuccino and caffè latte into a social culture all its own.

Another phenomenon is the "go" cup generation walking the streets of our major cities both morning and afternoon with paper or refillable commuter cups brimming with cappuccino and caffè latte, hot, cold, or flavored. Women's fashions include espresso, cappuccino and hazelnut in the color palette. Even the nationally syndicated comic strip character Brenda Starr has said, "Aarrgh! I need a caffè break. There's no problem that can't be improved with a shot of espresso."

Welcome to the espresso revolution in North America.

THE EVOLUTION OF ESPRESSO MACHINES

During the mid-1800's a variety of large steam-operated commercial machines were developed in France and Italy, using a brewing principle similar to the Moka. Tall and ornate boilers generated steam pressure to force water through a mechanical filter, producing large quantities of strong, pungent coffee.

In the early 1900's Luigi Bezzera patented a steam pressure system that incorporated a filter holder and delivery group that brewed a single serving of espresso at one time. Desiderio Pavoni acquired Mr. Bezzera's patent, and, in 1910, Pavoni began manufacturing these machines for commercial use in espresso bars and restaurants.

These machines developed 1 to 3 ATMS of pressure, which is relatively low compared to the amount of pressure used today. All of these machines relied solely on steam pressure from large boilers that heated water above boiling, scalding the coffee and extracting some of the bitter oils and acids from the grounds.

For more than 40 years the Italian caffè scene struggled along with this somewhat bitter brew until after WWII, when Achilles Gaggia patented and introduced the first piston lever machine. To espresso lovers, this development was equivalent to the moment Alexander Graham Bell asked "Are you there Mr. Watson?"

The piston lever machine was the first to produce espresso as we know it today. Pressure was developed by a spring loaded lever and piston, instead of steam pressure, eliminating the need to heat water above boiling to brew espresso. Two significant factors were the thermostatic control of the water brewing temperature and the ability to develop sufficient pressure with the piston lever to quickly force the water through a fine espresso grind.

Twelve years later, in 1961, Ernesto Valente developed the first commercial espresso machine, which replaced the piston lever with an electric centrifugal pump to provide the pressure. The centrifugal pump supplied constant pressure of 9 ATMS to force the water through the espresso grind. Valente also used a heat exchanger to simultaneously control the brewing temperature at 198°F and the steaming temperature at over 250°F.

The use of a pump eventually made it possible to develop commercial machines that would operate automatically at the touch of a button. This technology also spurred the development of pump-driven home espresso machines that closely duplicated the results achieved by the larger commercial equipment found in cafés and restaurants.

Several Italian espresso machine manufacturers began producing pump-driven espresso machines for home use in the 1960's. Because of size and cost limitations, home-use pump-driven espresso machines do not use the constant pressure centrifugal pump or heat exchanger used in commercial equipment. Instead, pump-driven espresso machines for the home rely on what is referred to as a reciprocal pump, which operates somewhat like a pulsing solenoid.

The centrifugal pump used in commercial equipment provides constant pressure at 9 ATMS or 132 psi. The reciprocal pump in home machines produces pulsing pressure from 9 to 17 ATMS (135 to 250 psi). As an object of comparison, the water pressure supplied by most city water systems for the average kitchen faucet is 35 psi. One atmosphere (ATM) equals 14.69 pounds per square inch (psi) of water pressure.

Other than the obvious difference in cost and size, one major difference between commercial and home-use machines is the "dwell time" or recovery period between brewing and steaming temperatures. Commercial equipment in operation more than 12 hours a day uses a heat exchanger or double boiler.

The centrifugal pump draws fresh water into the heat exchanger for brewing espresso, and steam is generated in a separate boiler available on demand, avoiding any dwell time. Pump-driven espresso machines for the home require a recovery period to adjust between the temperatures for brewing and generating steam.

As the evolution of the espresso machines continues, a new category of equipment is emerging referred to as "semi-commercial" machines. The term "semi-commercial" usually indicates a plug-in machine that is not permanently connected to a water supply and water is drawn from a refillable water reservoir. Manufacturers have addressed the dwell time situation by introducing scaled down heat exchanger systems, or double boilers and double thermal blocks, to avoid any dwell time in converting between brewing and steaming temperatures.

Semi-commercial machines are suitable for lower volume café service and will eventually find their home in the upscale kitchen of the espresso connoisseur.

HOME ESPRESSO EQUIPMENT

HOME ESPRESSO EQUIPMENT

A wide variety of home espresso and cappuccino equipment is available on the American market. More and more manufacturers are introducing sophisticated espresso machines, replacing the simpler stove-tops and non-pump units with semi-automatic and even fully automatic machines for home use. Most of this development is due to the increasing popularity of espresso and related beverages.

Regardless of their price, style or brand name, home espresso machines fall into three basic categories:

STOVE-TOP MAKERS
>   A. Gravity drip - Neopolitan
>   B. Pressure reverse drip - Moka
>   C. Pressure reverse drip with steam
>   D. Steamers for frothing milk

ELECTRIC NON-PUMP MACHINES
>   A. Steam boiler system
>   B. Piston-lever system

ELECTRIC PUMP ESPRESSO MACHINES
>   A. Pump boiler system
>   B. Pump thermal block system

STOVE-TOP MAKERS

OVERVIEW

Stove-top espresso makers are available in a variety of shapes and sizes at a relatively low price. These makers will produce a cup of good strong coffee, but it is virtually impossible to brew a serving of true espresso with crema in a stove-top maker.

The reason is twofold. Because there is little or no pressure developed in these stove-top systems, a coarse drip grind coffee must be used. And there is no thermostatic control over the water temperature, usually over 200°F, which scalds the coffee and extracts bitter oils.

In the case of the Moka-type stove-top a small amount of pressure is developed, approximately 1.5 ATM or 22 psi (pounds-per-square inch) of pressure. However, water is still heated above 200°F in order to develop the pressure, and the pressure is insufficient to force water through a fine grind.

NEOPOLITAN

Sometimes referred to as a macchinetta (little machine) or flip drip pot, the Neopolitan apparently originated in France during the mid-1800's and was quickly adapted by the Italians in Naples, hence the name Neopolitan. This stove-top system uses the same gravity brewing principle as any drip coffee maker. Water is heated in one chamber, inverted or flipped over a coffee chamber, and the water seeps through the coffee basket into a serving chamber. Neopolitans are usually available in sizes from two to 12-cup capacities.

Without pressure in the system, the Neopolitan stove-top relies on gravity to brew the coffee. A coarse grind must be used to enable the heated water to seep through the coffee basket into the serving chamber.

One suggestion for slightly improving the taste of this strong Italian coffee would be to invert the Neopolitan before the water in the heating chamber reaches a full boil. Another suggestion would be to heat water in a saucepan to just below boiling and to then pour the water into the coffee basket cylinder, which at least would eliminate a scalded coffee flavor.

STOVE-TOP PRESSURE MAKERS (Moka)

Developed in 1933 by Alfonso Bialetti, this system was an improvement over the Neopolitan because it developed slight pressure on the stove top. Sometimes called the Moka, the pressure reverse drip system operates under pressure supplied by boiling water in a sealed chamber.

Steam pressure, generated by heating water in the bottom chamber, forces water upward through a coffee basket, and an outlet tube releases brewed coffee into the top serving section. A coarse grind must be used, since the pressure developed is not sufficient to force the water through a fine espresso grind.

A rubber gasket seals the bottom boiling chamber to develop roughly 20 to 30 psi of pressure. A safety release valve prevents the build up of excessive steam pressure in the boiling chamber. The build up of too much pressure from a grind too fine for this type of machine could pop the safety release valve.

It is important to follow the manufacturer's instructions for cleaning the safety valve and replacing the rubber gasket. The Moka is usually available in aluminum or stainless steel in sizes from one to 12 cup capacities.

Again, it may help avoid a scalded coffee flavor to remove the Moka from the stove top before the unit reaches a full boil, which usually can be determined by opening the lid and watching the center coffee outlet for signs of steam being evacuated.

The 20 to 30 psi of steam pressure developed in a Moka stove-top maker compares to the 35 psi supplied to the average kitchen faucet. Pump-driven espresso machines for home use generate from 135 to 250 psi of pump pressure.

The Moka will brew a good cup of strong coffee, but the combination of a coarse grind and high heat will not produce an espresso with crema. Combined with a stove-top steamer, Moka-type coffee is a respectable base for cappuccino and caffe latte.

STOVE-TOP PRESSURE WITH STEAMING PROVISION

A variation of stove-top pressure makers incorporates the convenience of a steaming provision and offers a coffee control valve to regulate the flow of water through the ground coffee. A steam release valve controls the release of steam for steaming or frothing milk.

Most stove-top pressure systems with steam provisions have adjustable coffee baskets to brew from three to nine servings, using the same brewing principle as the Moka. Ample steam is generated on the stove top, sufficient to froth milk for a cappuccino-type drink using a strong drip coffee, not true espresso, as the base.

CAPPUCCINO & LATTE STEAMERS

Stove-top pressure systems that do not brew coffee but only generate steam for frothing milk are also available. These makers work quite well and may also be used to heat other beverages, like flavored steamers, hot apple cider or hot chocolate.

Although stove-top makers feature a safety pressure release valve, caution should be used due to the high heat and pressure developed. Always follow the manufacturer's instructions.

ELECTRIC NON-PUMP ESPRESSO MACHINES

Because of their lower price, electric non-pump espresso machines represent the largest selling category of espresso machines in North America.

Steam pressure is developed in a sealed boiler by raising the temperature of the water above 200°F. Considered by many to be a good entry level machine, there are certain limitations in terms of brewing café-quality espresso with crema. However, this type of machine provides ample steam generation for a very respectable cappuccino or caffè latte. Please refer to Chapter 5 for complete details on the electric non-pump system.

PISTON LEVER MACHINE

A classic in the industry, the piston lever system represented the first major break through in espresso machine technology. The piston lever was the first machine to produce an espresso serving with crema as we know it today.

Pulling down on the lever pressurizes the water by forcing a piston through the brewing chamber to fully extract the espresso flavor. Thermostats control the separate brewing and steaming temperatures.

The piston lever system will produce an excellent serving of café-quality espresso with crema and provides plentiful steam generation for frothing milk. However, consistent results from a piston lever machine are more dependent on the operator (Barista) than more modern push-button, pump-driven espresso machines. Please refer to Chapter 5 for complete details on the piston lever system.

PUMP-BOILER SYSTEM

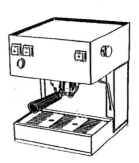

Similar in principle to the larger boiler systems used in commercial espresso equipment, the pump-boiler system for home use operates with a pump and heated water contained in a sealed boiler. The pump draws water from a reservoir into the boiler, and thermostats control the separate brewing and steaming temperatures.

The pump does not operate in the steam mode on a pump-boiler system, and encapsulated steam is released from the top of the boiler through the steam pipe only when the steam valve is open. A pump-boiler system will brew café-quality espresso with crema and provide excellent steam generation for cappuccino and lattes. Please refer to Chapter 5 for complete details on the pump-boiler espresso system.

PUMP THERMAL BLOCK

A relatively new innovation in espresso machine technology, the thermal block is a radiator-like device that replaces the boiler. Coiled channels in the thermal block contain the heating element that flash-heats the water to the separate brewing and steaming temperatures, which are controlled thermostatically.

Unlike the pump-boiler system, the pump operates in the steam mode on a pump thermal block system, and you can hear the pump pulsing water from the reservoir through the thermal block in the steam mode. A thermal block system will brew café-quality espresso with crema, and provide continuous steam for cappuccino and lattes. Please refer to Chapter 5 for complete details on the pump thermal block system.

COMBINATION MACHINES

Several espresso machine manufacturers now offer combination machines that provide an automatic drip coffee maker with the espresso/cappuccino feature in one combined unit. This type of combo system is a space saving appliance, convenient for home entertaining. A certain number of guests will prefer American drip coffee, while others may have developed a taste for espresso-related beverages.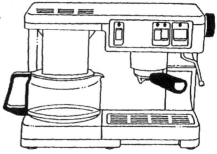

Combination units are available with either a non-pump or a pump-driven espresso system with an automatic drip coffee maker and are priced accordingly (pump vs. non-pump). In either case, the drip coffee and espresso functions operate independently or simultaneously. You may either brew just drip coffee or just espresso, or prepare both at the same time. (Note, you cannot simultaneously brew espresso and generate steam on any home unit without a heat exchanger or double boiler/thermal block).

SEMI-AUTOMATIC ESPRESSO MACHINES

Espresso machines classified as semi-automatic feature a built-in adjustable burr grinder that dispenses ground coffee into the filter holder.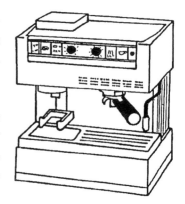

Some units electronically control the amount of coffee dosed into the filter holder so that the grinder dispenses either a single or double dose of pre-measured finely ground coffee.

The term semi-automatic indicates that the "user" is still involved in the process, and the coffee must be tamped in the coffee basket, the filter holder inserted into the brew head, and a switch pressed to brew single or double servings of espresso. Semi-automatic machines also have a provision for steaming.

FULLY AUTOMATIC ESPRESSO MACHINES

This term describes an espresso machine that does not have a filter holder and, at the push of a button, performs all of the basic brewing functions within the machine. The coffee is ground to a precise consistency in the built-in burr grinder and is automatically dosed into a tamping cylinder in the brewing assembly where the ground coffee is tamped. A regulated amount of heated water is pumped through the compressed coffee directly into the espresso cup(s). The machine then disposes of the used coffee grounds internally and is ready to start another brewing cycle automatically.

All of this happens at the simple touch of one button. Other than selecting the initial setting for the consistency of the grind and regulating the amount of water to flow through the brewing cylinder, it is a totally hands-free automatic brewing system.

Some fully automatic systems only brew one serving of espresso at one time, and others brew two servings simultaneously. This type of system usually features a grinder by-pass where pre-ground decaf coffee is introduced into the machine, and the brewing cycle bypasses the built-in grinder on this brewing cycle. All of these machines have a traditional steaming provision, although machines are now on the market with fully automatic steaming for complete cappuccino or caffè latte from start to finish at the push of a button!

COMMERCIAL ESPRESSO EQUIPMENT

Although this book is devoted to home espresso machines, there seems to be some interest in how home machines compare to commercial equipment in terms of operation. One significant difference is the ability to simultaneously brew espresso and generate steam. A commercial system eliminates any dwell time by maintaining two separate water supplies for brewing and steam.

Pump-Boiler System:

This system is similar in principle to the home pump-boiler system, except that the boiler is larger and usually constructed of copper or stainless steel. Commercial boiler machines use a large centrifugal pump which, in some cases, is inside the machine housing and, in other cases, is located below the machine in a separate compartment.

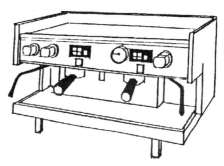

The water in the boiler is thermostatically maintained at the high steaming temperature, well above boiling, and the water used for brewing espresso is controlled below boiling within a heat exchanger or double boiler.

A separate plumbing system feeds the brew head that derives its heat source from the steam in the boiler system. In other words, the heated water in the boiler for steam is never used to brew espresso.

Commercial machines are often multi-group, which means anywhere from one to four or more brew heads and filter holders (called the delivery group) produce multiple servings of espresso at one time. Each delivery group has its own heat exchanger, and, because of the large size of the boiler, there is always ample steam for steaming and frothing milk.

Some commercial machines have the tall and ornate domes of the very early machines that housed a large steam boiler to develop pressure. With the advent of the centrifugal pump that delivers constant pressure at 9 ATM, some of the tall domes are actually empty and merely used as decoration.

Piston Lever System:

The variations to this configuration eliminate the centrifugal pump in the brewing system in favor of the down stroke of the piston lever providing pressure, or an automatic spring loaded piston is used where the pressure develops on the up stroke (return) of the lever. Many professional Baristas prefer the interaction with the lever, allowing them to control the extraction of the espresso.

COFFEE GRINDERS

COFFEE GRINDERS

One of the most critical elements in producing café-quality espresso is the consistency and uniformity of the ground coffee in the filter holder. You can invest in the most expensive espresso machine and the finest and freshest coffee, but, unless the beans are ground to the proper consistency for your machine, the finished product will be disappointing.

If you buy your coffee pre-ground from a specialty coffee retailer, you should not only check the freshness of their coffee but also let them know the type of espresso machine you use at home. This will enable them to grind to the correct consistency and fineness of the grind for your machine (stove-top, electric non-pump, or pump-driven machine). Once you have established the correct grinder setting on their grinder for your machine, note this setting so that you can instruct the retailer each time you buy your pre-ground espresso to grind at that setting on their grinder. It may take some trial and error, but the reward is well worth the effort.

Remember that it is the fineness of the grind that provides resistance to the water ensuring complete saturation of the "bed" of coffee in the filter holder. If you own a pump-driven or piston lever machine, you may eventually invest in a burr grinder. Whole bean espresso coffee has a longer shelf life than pre-ground; in addition, pre-ground coffee loses a good portion of its flavor after being exposed to air and humidity for only a few hours. The proper grind for your particular machine is critical, and, in the long run, a quality burr grinder is worth the investment.

BLADE GRINDERS

Electric blade grinders whirl two blades at high speed which literally knock the coffee beans to pieces. Blade grinders work well for stove-top and drip coffee makers. For espresso, however, a consistent, fine grind is required.

Because you cannot control the whirling blades of a blade grinder, there is no consistency to the grind. The whirling blades knock the coffee beans into both larger pieces and partial dust or powder. This powdery grind may clog the small perforations in the coffee basket of the filter holder, completely restricting the flow of water through the espresso grind.

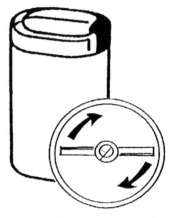

The whirling blades also generate heat that can dissipate some of the delicate oils and flavor essential to brewing espresso with crema.

Relatively inexpensive and quite efficient for preparing a coarser grind for stove-top or drip coffee makers, blade grinders are not recommended for use with a pump-driven or piston lever espresso machine.

HAND BURR GRINDERS

Until the advent of electric grinders and pre-ground vacuum packed coffee, every household had a hand-operated burr grinder. Almost everyone's great- or great-great grandmother started the morning chores by placing a box grinder between her knees and turning the crank to prepare the morning's wake up brew. The sound and aroma of the coffee mill ritual started the day for generations of people throughout the world.

There are two basic models: one called a box grinder, usually a wooden box with a crank at the top and a drawer to collect the ground coffee, and the other a wall-hung model with a cast iron hopper and metal container to collect the ground coffee.

The hand grinder is a manual version of the electric burr grinder and an extension of the grain mill and mortar and pestle. Whole coffee beans are ground between two corrugated steel disks, or burrs, one stationary and the other rotating. The crank handle provides the control over the rotation and features an adjustment nut that sets the distance between the burrs to control the consistency of the grind.

A good quality hand burr grinder will provide a consistent, fine grind for espresso; however, the manual operation requires some patience.

ELECTRIC BURR GRINDERS

Electric burr grinders feature grinding adjustments from coarse to very fine. Opposing burrs shave the whole beans to a uniform grind by the chosen index setting or distance between the burrs. The top burr is stationary and the bottom burr rotates.

Burr grinders minimize heat in the grinding process, and some of the more expensive burr grinders feature a gear reduction motor that slows the rotation of the burrs to further reduce heat and dissipation of volatile oils in the beans.

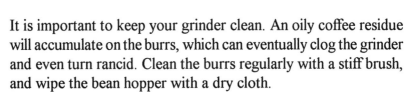

Burr grinders for home use usually have a flat or slightly tapered set of corrugated burrs. More expensive or commercial versions of the burr grinder have a deeper taper or conical shape for an even more precise adjustment and grind.

It is important to keep your grinder clean. An oily coffee residue will accumulate on the burrs, which can eventually clog the grinder and even turn rancid. Clean the burrs regularly with a stiff brush, and wipe the bean hopper with a dry cloth.

Most burr grinders dispense ground coffee into a collection chamber, and ground coffee is spooned from the chamber into the coffee basket.

Some burr grinders feature an espresso doser with a lever that sweeps a pre-measured dose of the ground coffee directly into the espresso filter holder. One sweep of the lever doses roughly seven grams of coffee into the filter holder for a single serving, two sweeps for a double serving.

Until recently, there were few electric home burr grinders available in America, and those that were available for home use were relatively expensive. As a result of the espresso explosion, more and more burr grinders are available at a wide variety of price points.

It should be noted that some inexpensive burr grinders may not grind beans fine enough for a pump-driven or piston lever machine.

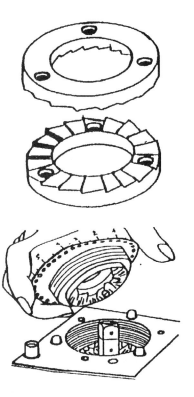

In addition, as in the case of an electric blade grinder, an inconsistent grind of partial powder will not allow the complete extraction of the full espresso flavor from the ground coffee.

Before investing in a quality burr grinder, ask your retailer to demonstrate the grinder in order to determine whether the grind will be sufficiently fine, but not too fine, and of a consistent grind for your espresso machine.

A burr grinder will not only contribute to your enjoyment of espresso but will also improve the flavor of drip coffee. As an additional benefit, you will eventually save money, since whole beans retain their flavor much longer than pre-ground coffee.

HELPFUL HINTS FOR BURR GRINDER USERS

1. An espresso roast can range from slightly oily to very oily, and very oily beans tend to stick together. As the quantity and weight of the beans in the hopper diminishes, it may require a little coaxing to feed all of the beans into the grinding mechanism.

A slight shake of the grinder should drop any remaining beans, or stir the beans to make sure they are feeding properly into the grinding mechanism. This problem is even more pronounced if whole beans with an oily surface have been stored in the refrigerator or freezer, since the oil coagulates and the beans cling together.

2. Many burr grinders "spit" ground coffee onto the counter top, but there does not seem to be any way to avoid ground coffee residue unless you step up to one of the more expensive commercial-type burr grinders.

3. If your grinder includes an espresso doser attachment and you are only preparing two or three servings of espresso, consider not using the doser attachment. It takes a good portion of ground coffee to fill the doser compartment, and pre-ground coffee will lose its flavor overnight in the grinder once it is ground and exposed to oxygen.

For related information, refer to the sections on grinding under "Preparing Espresso" and "Storage of Coffee".

CARE AND MAINTENANCE
OF A BURR GRINDER

A burr grinder should be cleaned frequently, since the accumulation of oils from the coffee beans and ground coffee can turn rancid and contaminate the coffee flavor.

The bean hopper and doser should be washed frequently, by hand, in mild soapy water and rinsed thoroughly so as not to impart a soap residue to the coffee flavor. The burrs should be cleaned periodically with a stiff brush to remove any oils and gummy coffee residue. Special grinder brushes are now available from many specialty coffee retailers.

Please bear in mind that if you grind flavored beans in a burr grinder, the flavor will be retained in the grinding mechanism and will be imparted to subsequent grindings of unflavored beans.

Eventually the burrs will become dull and need replacing, but this would be after more than five years of normal home use. In a commercial environment, the grinder burrs are usually replaced after 600 pounds of coffee have been ground.

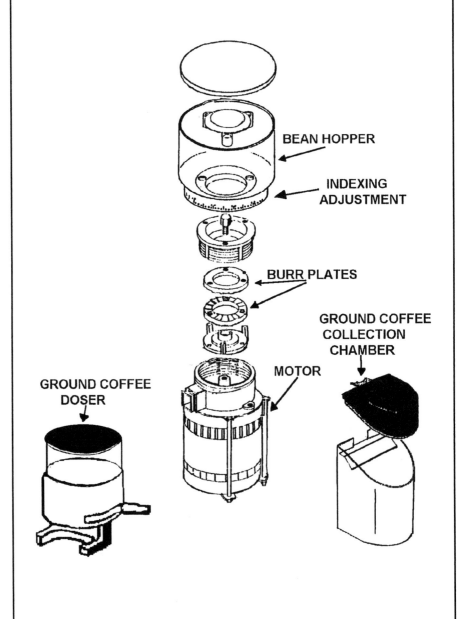

ANATOMY OF A
BURR GRINDER

BEAN HOPPER

INDEXING
ADJUSTMENT

BURR PLATES

GROUND COFFEE
COLLECTION
CHAMBER

MOTOR

GROUND COFFEE
DOSER

ESPRESSO
FROM
BEANS
TO
BREW

MARVELOUS, MYSTERIOUS COFFEE

What an incredible journey this brew has made from the *Coffea arabica* discovered growing wild in central Ethiopia to the espresso and cappuccino consumed today in glitzy coffeehouses all across North America.

Coffee is the second largest commodity traded in the world, second only to oil. Coffee grows in more than 50 countries throughout the world, and the economies of most coffee-producing countries are completely dependent on this commodity. Coffee is a fascinating subject meriting its own book, and several good ones have been written.

The history of coffee is buried in fact and fable, spiced with tales of romance and political intrigue, all of which adds to the mystique of the bean.

A BRIEF HISTORY

The best known legend surrounding the discovery of coffee concerns Kaldi, an Ethiopian goat herder who one day found his goats acting like kids. They had been eating red berries from a shiny, dark-leafed shrub growing on the hillside. Kaldi tried the berries and pranced with the goats. An abbot watched this activity and gave some of the berries to neighboring monks, who prayed all night without falling asleep.

More likely, coffee was first noticed by wandering tribesmen known to have eaten the berries crushed to a pulp, mixed with animal fats, and rolled into balls of food. Later, the berries were made into a broth with water. Roasting and grinding became popular in Arabia by the 13th century.

Supposedly, Coffea arabica crossed the Red Sea to Yemen during the Ethiopian invasion of Southern Arabia in 515 AD, and the Ethiopians ruled Yemen for fifty years. Cultivation of coffee in Arabia was recorded in 575, when the Persians invaded and ended the Ethiopian reign.

WHERE COFFEE IS GROWN

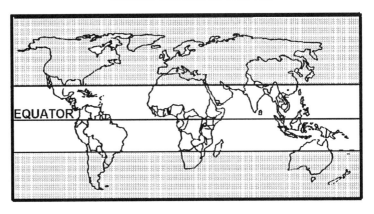

Arabians first used coffee as a medicine, and the medicinal aspect remained associated with coffee for centuries. It was used as a beverage during religious and meditation ceremonies. Eventually coffee moved to Middle Eastern coffeehouses and was cultivated in Persia, Egypt, North Africa and Turkey. Coffeehouses were then considered to be dens of iniquity.

Apparently the Arabs sought to control the export of coffee by only allowing parched or boiled beans that would not germinate to be exported. The traditional pilgrimages to Mecca ended this monopoly when some of the pilgrims carried the cherished beans back to their homelands.

Being great travelers, Venetians may have been the first Europeans to acquire coffee. Medicinal qualities were still being stressed in 1580 when coffee was brought from Egypt. Some Italian wine growers became alarmed at possible competition, and they petitioned the Pope to ban coffee. But, when the Pope tasted it, he enjoyed it so much he gave it his blessing.

The Dutch recognized the value of coffee and cultivated it in the East Indies, most notably the island of Java. The Dutch presented Louis XIV of France with a valuable coffee tree. The French cultivated coffee in the West Indies from Martinique, after a perilous journey where only one of three coffee trees survived. Another coffee tree was spirited to Brazil, which became one of the largest coffee-producing countries in the world.

By the 17th century, the seeds of one legendary tree became a worldwide passion. Records show coffee was first served in 1668 in New York as a beverage brewed from beans and sweetened with honey. Soon all of the colonies had founded coffeehouses. John Adams and Paul Revere allegedly plotted the American Revolution at the Green Dragon Coffee House in Boston. For hundreds of years, coffee supplies were abundant.

Eventually, coffee consumption all over the world was beginning to deplete the available supplies. After WWII, the quality of coffee in the United States declined and, by the 1960's, less expensive robusta beans were used in high-volume commercial blends. The electric coffee percolator popular at that time further deteriorated the coffee flavor.

An example of the volatility of coffee as an important worldwide commodity is the disaster that struck in 1975, when a sudden frost in Brazil destroyed millions of trees. Shortly after, civil war in Angola cut their harvest; floods in Colombia destroyed trees; an earthquake in Guatemala depleted the crop, and many other Central American countries were forced to deal with the disease called coffee rust. Coffee prices soared.

In spite of higher prices, coffee sales remained reasonably stable. The higher quality "gourmet" coffee market began to spread throughout North America in the late 1970's. A significant development in the industry was the tremendous growth in the number of specialty coffee roasters and retailers during the 1980's that continues today. This phenomenon is stimulated by the more recent interest in espresso and espresso-related beverages.

CULTIVATING COFFEE

Arabica:

The Coffea arabica tree is very sensitive and requires an almost perfect balance of sunshine, shade and rain. The differences in flavor are caused by variations in soil, climate, humidity and the amount of annual rain fall. The tree grows naturally to a height of 30 feet but is usually cultivated at six to ten feet to make harvesting easier and help increase the yield.

Coffea arabica is referred to as "high grown" coffee because the arabica tree grows at elevations above 2,000 feet, producing only two pounds of coffee per tree within three to five years of planting.

Robusta:

Coffea canephora (robusta) was discovered growing wild in the Belgian Congo, now Zaire. Robusta grows at lower altitudes, from sea level to 2,000 feet, and is cultivated for the hardiness and fertility of the tree. Each tree produces enough fruit for four pounds of coffee within two to three years of planting. Robusta beans are smaller and rounder with twice the caffeine of arabicas.

There is no comparison in flavor between arabica and robusta beans, and robustas are mainly used for commercial (high-volume) blends and soluble (instant) coffees.

HARVESTING

The coffee tree has dark green, leathery, oblong leaves with small, white, fragrant flowers. The clustered fruit of the tree turns green from six to nine months after flowering and then ripens to a red berry that resembles a cherry (coffee berries are called cherries).

Growing coffee is a very labor-intensive industry. The cherries must be picked quickly, as they ripen over a period of days. The cherries are often picked by hand as they ripen, and pickers return to a tree five or six times. One 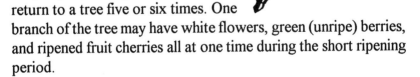 branch of the tree may have white flowers, green (unripe) berries, and ripened fruit cherries all at one time during the short ripening period.

Machines used to strip the coffee tree of ripened berries cannot discriminate between green and red berries, or even flowers and branch bits. Hand-picking coffee is the preferred method and obviously more expensive.

PROCESSING THE BEAN

The actual red berry contains two seeds with flat sides facing each other. These are the coffee beans. The outside skin of the berry contains a fruit pulp, and each bean is wrapped in an outer parchment and an inner silver skin. Occasionally, nature provides a single round bean, called a peaberry, instead of two flat beans per cherry.

A delicate stage is processing the coffee cherries to remove the outer husk and reveal the beans. The cherries are processed in one of two methods, or a combination of both: a wet method (washed) before the cherries have dried, or a dry method (unwashed) where the cherries are dried naturally. The process chosen often depends on the availability of water in the coffee-producing region. Regardless of the method (wet or dry), the care taken in processing the cherries has a profound impact on the quality and final cost of the beans.

SKIN
PULP
PARCHMENT
SILVER SKIN
COFFEE BEAN

The wet or washed method is a complex process that removes the outer layers of the cherry by soaking the cherries in tanks for 12 to 24 hours. The delicate fermentation process takes place before the beans have dried. The beans are thoroughly washed, drained, and dried in the sun or by mechanical driers that provide a current of hot air. Hulling or milling machines remove the last protective parchment and silver skin. The wet or washed method is more expensive and is said to be superior in providing a more consistent flavor.

The dry method is an older process, where the cherries are spread in the sun to dry naturally in one to two weeks and raked several times a day to protect them from moisture. Fermentation takes place while the beans are drying, and the outer layers are allowed to shrivel around the beans. The dried hull is removed by milling machines.

Unless the cherries are hand-picked, the dry method is considered inferior because it also processes cherries that have not fully ripened, providing a more variable flavor. However, some of the world's most interesting varietals are dry processed beans.

GRADING

Grading is the step in the process that establishes the value of the green beans eventually sold to roasters. The beans are sorted for size by hand or by a shaking machine. The grade of a particular bean will vary by region, and no two crops are identical. By sizing and grading the beans, defects are discovered. As an example, broken beans are considered a defect because they roast darker and can negatively affect an entire batch of roast.

After grading, the beans are bagged for export to roasters. Straight coffees in the green bean stage are called varietals, and it is the roasting process that brings out the subtle characteristics of each varietal.

DECAFFEINATED COFFEE

Contrary to popular belief, the "jolt" often associated with espresso by the uninitiated is related to the intense flavor, not the caffeine content. Arabica beans contain half the caffeine of robustas used in commercial blends for drip coffee. In addition, an espresso roast is darkened by roasting longer, which further reduces the caffeine content.

Most specialty coffee retailers offer decaffeinated espresso, a boon for those affected by caffeine. For a coffee to be labeled "decaffeinated", at least 97% of the caffeine must be removed. The extra steps and handling involved in the decaffeination process are costly. Also, decaffeinated beans tend to roast darker and are more difficult to roast. Therefore, decaf coffee is more expensive.

It is a challenge to remove the caffeine from the beans and not remove the coffee flavor. The direct and indirect use of solvents in decaffeinating coffee have proponents and critics for every method. Different coffee varietals have different caffeine contents, and caffeine is water soluble. By soaking the green coffee beans in water, solvents are used to separate the caffeine from the water. The water with the coffee flavor is added back to the beans with at least 97% of the caffeine removed.

A survey in 1980 raised health questions about the various solvents used to decaffeinate coffee, at the same time the Swiss patented a water process using charcoal or carbon filters, instead of solvents, to separate the caffeine from the water. The health risks in the original survey were found to be negligible, but sales of Swiss water-processed decaffeinated coffee soared.

It is estimated that 25% of coffee sales today are of decaffeinated coffee, and technology continues to improve the process, which now includes "chemical-free" and "naturally decaffeinated" methods.

ORGANIC COFFEE

Organic beans are certified by U.S. government or independent agencies to be cultivated in areas free of pesticides and chemicals in the soil used to improve a coffee yield. Professionals debate the organic issue, from questioning the certification process to claiming organic beans lack flavor. Organic coffees are more expensive and growing in popularity among the health conscious and environmentally concerned.

THE ESPRESSO BLEND

Blending is the mixing of two or more straight coffees, usually after roasting. Anywhere from three to eight straight coffees are blended, either by the roaster or a specialty coffee retailer. The blend and roast of the whole bean are a matter of personal taste.

Three very broad geographical groups of coffee are:

Central & South American
East Africa & Yemen
Indonesian & Pacific Islands

Each blend has its own taste characteristics based on the origin of the beans and how they are roasted. The blending of straight coffees provides the final nuance of flavor, and the roastmaster enhances the subtle characteristics of each group in the roasting process.

There are virtually hundreds of different blends developed by coffee roasters and specialty coffee retailers. Discuss the many different blends with your local roaster or retailer, and experiment freely with different combinations to add variety to your espresso cuisine.

THE ESPRESSO ROAST

The roasting process forces moisture out of the bean and brings volatile oils closer to the surface of the bean. The essence of the espresso flavor is in these delicate oils. The darker the roast, the longer the bean was roasted, and a dark roast can have less caffeine than a lighter roast. As the high heat of the roaster forces moisture out of the bean, the bean expands but the weight diminishes.

There is no precise standardized terminology used to describe the coffee roast. Viennese, Italian, French, and American are not the origin of the bean but instead refer to the degree of roasting and that depends on the standards of the roaster.

In some regions, a French roast would indicate the darkest possible roast, whereas in other regions an Italian roast may indicate the darkest roast.

The degree of roast is totally dependent on the roaster, and roasters take great pride in their art. The roasting process determines the character of any coffee flavor. Espresso with crema reveals the roastmaster's expertise, but the preferred espresso roast is still a matter of personal taste.

There are three basic types of espresso roasts, any combination of which may be used to prepare espresso:

1.) Full City Roast - a light dark roast, medium brown in color with a dry surface and mild, smooth taste

2.) Medium Dark Roast - a darker brown color with a slightly oily surface and fuller flavor

3.) Dark Roast - the darkest color and shiniest surface, with a sharper, intense flavor

An espresso roast suggests the darkest bean and a bolder taste, but there is no official espresso blend or degree of roast. In central Europe, espresso is often brewed with a light, dark roast, much lighter than the very dark "espresso" or "Italian" roast that has become popular in many regions of the United States.

Experiment in selecting a blend and roast, as long as the beans are fresh and ground to the right consistency for your espresso machine.

THE ESPRESSO GRIND

The right espresso grind provides the resistance to the water under pressure that is essential to extracting the heart of espresso flavor.

This vital step in preparing café-quality espresso may require a period of trial and error to fine-tune the consistency of the grind to your particular espresso machine.

The beans must be ground fine, but not too fine. If the grind is too fine, a powder grind, water cannot flow through the grind even under pressure. A powder grind feels like flour when rubbed between your fingers. A fine grind should feel gritty, like salt.

If the water flows very slowly, or not at all, the grind is too fine for your machine. Another variable is the quantity of coffee used and the pressure applied when tamping the coffee in the coffee basket. A more powerful machine develops greater pressure and takes a finer grind.

However, if the grind is too fine, or the coffee tamped too compactly, the water under pressure in the brew head will not be able to flow through the grind, and coffee may spurt from around the filter holder.

Water follows the path of least resistance, especially water under pressure. If the grind is too coarse, the water will flow too quickly through the coffee basket and not have contact with the entire dose of espresso in the coffee basket.

The proper grind for your particular espresso machine is critical to extracting a crema espresso. If you own a pump-driven machine and burr grinder, you will need to test the fineness of the grind at different indexes on the grinder before determining the optimum grind for your machine. True Baristas are known to adjust the proven grind for their preferred roast depending on the humidity factor in the air on certain days.

Eventually you may determine the cost of a burr grinder is worth the investment, because whole beans retain their freshness longer than pre-ground coffee, and you can adjust the grind to suit your pump-driven or piston lever machine.

PURCHASING ESPRESSO COFFEE

The quality of your espresso will only be as good as the freshness and quality of the beans you buy. Ideally, coffee should be purchased as close to the actual roaster as possible.

How often a retailer's whole bean stock is turned will be an indication of the freshness of the roast. Whole beans retain their flavor and freshness from only two to four weeks after roasting, depending upon how they are stored. Whole beans from a specialty coffee retailer are usually fresher than beans sold at a supermarket.

When purchasing coffee, important considerations are the quality of the beans or where the green beans originated, the degree or length of time they were roasted, when they were roasted, and the blend. Specialty coffee retailers have the knowledge and interest in your satisfaction that make it well worth the effort to locate them.

If you do not own a burr grinder, when purchasing fresh ground espresso from your specialty coffee retailer, let them know whether you have a pump-driven machine. Once the proper grind for your machine has been determined, note the index setting on their grinder for future purchases.

When purchasing fresh ground espresso from a specialty coffee retailer, consider buying smaller quantities more often, which will also give you an opportunity to experiment with their "house" blends.

Keep in mind that once the beans are ground, more surface area is exposed to air, and the flavor evaporation process begins immediately. Unprotected pre-ground coffee will lose some of its flavor within two to three hours after grinding.

You can delay this staling process for several days if you immediately store pre-ground coffee in an air-tight container made of glass or ceramic with a rubber seal.

Buy a small air-tight container especially for your coffee, small enough for the amount of coffee leaving the least amount of oxygen in the sealed container. Storing one half pound of pre-ground coffee in a one-quart container leaves a great deal of oxygen in the container that will rapidly dissipate flavor.

STORING ESPRESSO COFFEE

The roasting process forces moisture out of the bean and brings the delicate oils closer to the surface of the bean. These volatile oils are highly susceptible to odors. An air-tight glass or ceramic container with a rubber seal is recommended for storing whole beans and pre-ground coffee.

Fresh roasted whole beans begin to dissipate flavor rapidly, and pre-ground coffee begins to dissipate flavor immediately. Oxygen, light and humidity are the culprits that zap the flavor from freshly roasted (and ground) coffee. Use the right sized container for the amount of coffee you intend to store, so that there is the least amount of oxygen in the sealed container.

The storage of coffee is another controversial issue among professionals. Some recommend freezer storage in a sealed container to prolong the freshness of whole beans. Others believe the moisture generated by the refrigerator or freezer deteriorates the flavor.

Beans or pre-ground coffee stored in the refrigerator can deteriorate quickly, since moisture and odors will find their way even through a sealed container by condensation. In addition, darker roasted, oilier beans that are refrigerated tend to gum up in a burr grinder.

The freshness of whole beans can be prolonged by freezer storage if the quantity of beans is no more than you plan to use in 30 days. If you must freeze your excess coffee beans, try to remove as much air from the container as possible, and hope for the best. Take a look inside of a frozen package of green beans, and you will see the crystallized condensation inside the package even though the package was sealed.

We recommend storing whole beans and pre-ground coffee in an air-tight glass or ceramic container with a rubber seal, the right size for the amount of coffee you will be storing, and that it be kept in a cool, dry and dark area. And consider buying only the amount of coffee you plan to use within two weeks for the freshest flavor.

IN-STORE PACKAGING OPTIONS

PLAIN BROWN BAG

Most retailers package beans or pre-ground coffee in a plain brown or decorated bag. This bag affords no protection against humidity, oxygen or moisture, all of which are enemies of freshly roasted coffee. Your purchase should be immediately transferred to an air-tight container.

VACUUM PACKED CAN

Because freshly roasted and freshly ground coffee release carbon dioxide gas, the coffee must be degassed (exposed to air) before it is vacuum packed. In the case of vacuum packed beans, the degassing process can take up to several days (for ground coffee up to several hours), which, unfortunately, dissipates some of the volatile oils that contain most of the desirable coffee flavor. If coffee were not degassed before vacuum packaging in a can, the pressure would cause the can to burst.

Many brands of pre-ground vacuum packed coffee in cans are a coarse grind for stove-top or drip coffee systems. Therefore, this grind may be too coarse for a pump-driven espresso machine. Some roasters specifically mark their pre-ground vacuum packed cans as a fine espresso grind for a pump-driven espresso machine, so be sure to read the description to determine the right grind for your machine.

ONE-WAY VALVE BAGS

This type of packaging is a great improvement, since it allows the carbon dioxide gas to escape through a one-way valve without allowing oxygen to enter the package and dissipate flavor. This one-way valve system allows freshly roasted coffee to be packaged immediately and extends the shelf-life of the coffee up to three months or more.

Once the package is opened, there is no protection to prolong the freshness of the beans or the pre-ground coffee, and the coffee should be immediately transferred to an air-tight container.

VACUUM (BRICK) PACK

This type of packaging is a relatively new innovation making it possible to pack freshly roasted beans and pre-ground coffee in a heavy plastic film, shaped like a brick and almost as hard. This type of package is usually sold in 250 gram or 500 gram packs with a shelf-life of six to 12 months. Once the brick pack is opened the staling process begins immediately, and proper storage is highly recommended.

PODS

Another relatively recent system, the pod concept, adds convenience as well as extended shelf-life. Pods resemble circular tea bags and usually contain a fine grind espresso coffee.

Pods are designed to fit into the filter holder coffee basket of most pump-driven machines, and you can brew from one to two servings by placing one pod or two on top of one another in the coffee basket.

The flavor of the ground coffee in the pod will dissipate quickly unless the pod is sealed in an individual foil envelope. With pods protected in this fashion, the shelf-life could be more than 12 months. Pods are usually available in both regular and decaffeinated blends. Although pods tend to circumvent the theatrics of producing the perfect espresso, they can be very handy for spontaneous entertaining.

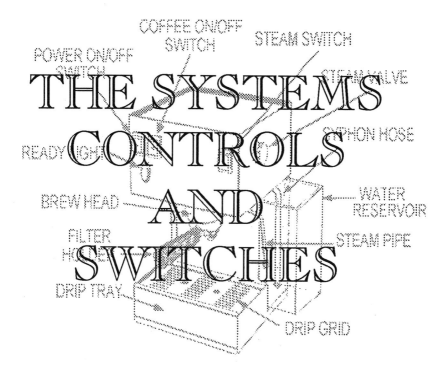

THE SYSTEMS
CONTROLS
AND
SWITCHES

POWER ON/OFF SWITCH

COFFEE ON/OFF SWITCH

STEAM SWITCH

STEAM VALVE

SIPHON HOSE

READY LIGHT

BREW HEAD

WATER RESERVOIR

FILTER HOLDER

STEAM PIPE

DRIP TRAY

DRIP GRID

ELECTRIC NON-PUMP ESPRESSO MACHINES

Electric non-pump espresso machines represent the largest selling category of espresso machines in the number of units sold in North America. They are lower in price compared to more sophisticated pump-driven boiler or thermal block machines, and, for that reason, this type of machine is considered by many to be an entry-level machine.

Most electric non-pump espresso machines have good steaming capabilities and will produce a very respectable cappuccino or caffè latte. But they do have certain limitations in connection with producing café-quality espresso with crema.

The technical difference between a non-pump and pump-driven machine is that the non-pump machine relies on the steam pressure developed in a boiler by heating water above 200°F. Water pressure developed in this manner is considerably less than the pressure developed in a pump-driven (boiler or thermal block) or piston lever system.

The pressure developed in a non-pump machine is approximately 3 ATMS (44 psi) compared to the 9 to 17 ATMS (135 to 250 psi) of pressure developed by a pump-driven espresso system.

Full-bodied espresso with crema can only be extracted with a fine espresso grind, and it requires at least 9 ATMS (135 psi) of pressure in order to force the heated water through a densely packed grind and fully extract all of the espresso coffee flavor.

In addition to the lack of sufficient pressure, the scalding point of espresso coffee is 199°F. Water in the non-pump boiler is heated over 200°F, and scalding coffee extracts bitter oils from the grind which break down the colloids that develop crema.

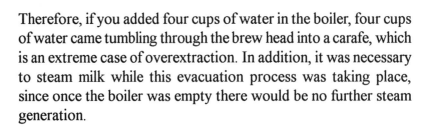

The earlier versions of these non-pump machines were difficult to operate, because there was no way to stop the flow of heated water through the brew head.

Therefore, if you added four cups of water in the boiler, four cups of water came tumbling through the brew head into a carafe, which is an extreme case of overextraction. In addition, it was necessary to steam milk while this evacuation process was taking place, since once the boiler was empty there would be no further steam generation.

Newer versions of the electric non-pump espresso machine feature a Coffee On/Off valve which controls the brewing for one or two servings of espresso and still leaves enough water in the boiler for generating steam.

With this improvement, and in spite of the high temperature, it is possible to produce a reasonably good cup of espresso as the base for a very respectable cappuccino or caffè latte.

It may take a little practice to fine-tune your espresso brewing and frothing skills on an electric non-pump espresso machine, but trial and error will prevail. You may wish to experiment with the consistency of the ground coffee to improve the flavor extraction, but do not use a grind too fine, since it will completely block the flow of water through the filter holder.

Once all of the water in the boiler has dissipated by brewing espresso and generating steam, it is necessary to turn off the machine and allow the unit to cool completely before removing the pressure cap to refill the boiler for additional servings of espresso or generating steam. During the cool-down period, always depressurize the boiler by opening the steam valve to relieve all of the remaining pressure.

We urge you to carefully review the manufacturer's instruction manual, since each of these machines has its own operating safety features, and, in many cases, they provide a specific formula for refilling the boiler for additional espresso servings and frothing milk.

IMPORTANT:

Please keep in mind that an electric non-pump espresso machine is a pressurized boiler system. Under no circumstances should you attempt to loosen or remove the pressure cap until you have released all of the pressure in the boiler through the steam pipe and allowed the machine to cool down completely.

PISTON LEVER
ESPRESSO MACHINE

The piston lever espresso machine is impressive and considered a classic in both the commercial and home-use categories. The concept was so revolutionary that Achilles Gaggia was able to obtain a patent after WWII on the piston lever principle.

Until the advent of the electric pump-driven espresso machine in 1961, the piston lever was the only system that developed high pressure in the brewing chamber without heating the water above 200°F. This enabled full extraction of the fine espresso grind in individual servings without high heat scalding the espresso flavor.

The trend in espresso bars today is toward a hands-free push-button machine as opposed to the highly personalized touch of an espresso master (Barista) using a piston lever.

But many espresso bar owners still insist on a piston lever machine, claiming it gives them the feel and touch required to produce a perfectly extracted espresso with crema.

Two types of piston lever machines are available commercially. One applies the pressure on the down stroke of the lever and the second where the down stroke merely compresses a heavy-duty spring that applies even pressure on the up stroke (return) of the lever.

The piston lever systems for home use available on the American market today are very efficient, high quality espresso machines, still considered by many to be a work of art. Piston lever machines are available in a chrome, copper or brass finish adorned with functionally operating pressure gauges, water level tubes, knobs and controls and a steam and hot water pipe.

Water is heated in a sealed boiler and flows into the piston chamber when the lever is in the up position. Pulling down on the lever forces the piston down through the chamber compressing the heated water, creating the pressure to force the water through a fine espresso grind.

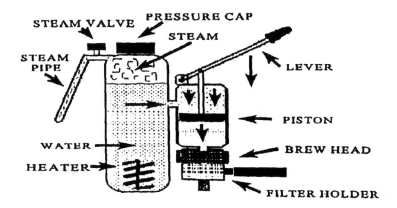

A thermostat controls the water temperature for brewing espresso. In the steam mode, the water is superheated to generate steam at the top of the boiler, released through the steam vent when the steam valve is opened.

A piston lever machine will produce café-quality espresso and generate ample steam. However, the final result is much more dependent on the skills of the operator in application of the pressure to the piston lever than push-button, pump-driven espresso machines.

ELECTRIC PUMP-DRIVEN ESPRESSO MACHINES

If you are in pursuit of the ultimate espresso experience, you will need a pump-driven (or piston lever) machine. The elusive crema can only be produced under certain controlled conditions. A properly brewed espresso with crema is the base for any number of espresso-related beverages.

The many different elements required to properly extract a true crema espresso include quality and freshness of the coffee, fineness of the grind, power of the espresso machine, controlled temperatures, tamping, timing, even the quality of the water.

The entire process, in our opinion, begins with an electric pump-driven (or piston lever) espresso machine. However, even purchasing an expensive piece of equipment does not assure that you will achieve café-quality espresso and cappuccino unless you fine-tune your espresso-making skills. Patience, trial and error will reward you with a skill that few Americans possess, and the lifelong pleasure of enjoying real espresso with crema at home.

PUMP PRESSURE

The pump used in home espresso equipment is a reciprocal (pulsing) pump that delivers varying pressure measured in atmospheres (ATM) and pounds per square inch (psi). One (1) ATM equals 14.69 psi.

Depending on its size, the pump pressure ranges from 9 to 17 ATM or 135 to 250 psi, depending on the machine used and the power of its pump.

Commercial espresso machines use a larger centrifugal pump that delivers a constant 9 ATM of pressure. The pump used in home espresso equipment is an in-line solenoid reciprocal pump rated from 50 to 70 watts.

The use of a fine espresso grind tamped in the coffee basket of the filter holder, inserted in the brew head, creates the resistance to the water forced through the grind under pump pressure to extract only the "heart" of the espresso flavor. The pump develops pressure in the brew head and filter holder (called the delivery group) and pulses water through the grind.

A more powerful pump will accept a finer espresso grind, and it is the fineness of the grind that creates the resistance to the water under pump pressure. Water follows the path of least resistance, and a fine grind forces the water to fully saturate the coffee.

Several new filter holder systems are available that provide further resistance to the water and build additional pressure in the delivery group, ensuring full saturation of the coffee and improving the crema. These devices are also more forgiving of an imperfect grind.

While the water is in contact with the coffee, the oils in the espresso grind form colloids that result in the crema that encrusts the top of a properly brewed espresso serving. Non-pump electric espresso machines generate an average of 3 ATM or 44 psi, which is insufficient pressure to force the water through a fine espresso grind.

PUMP BOILER SYSTEM

This system is similar in principle to commercial equipment used in coffee bars and restaurants. The water is pumped from the water reservoir into the boiler, where it is heated to below boiling (192-197°F) for brewing espresso.

A status or ready light will indicate when the water has reached the correct espresso brewing temperature, and a thermostat will maintain this temperature until you are ready to brew espresso.

The ready light may cycle on and off during operation, which is normal and indicates that the heating element is cycling to maintain the correct brewing temperature.

When the steam switch is activated, the heating element switches to a high-heat setting, and the water in the boiler is superheated from 250-270°F. A ready light indicates when the correct temperature for steaming has been reached. However, not all machines have a ready light for the steam mode, and the time required to superheat the system must be estimated. If the system has not reached the optimum steaming temperature, the first burst of steam may be weak and watery.

Steam accumulates in the top of the boiler and is not released through the steam vent until the steam valve (knob or lever) is opened. A second thermostat maintains the high heat setting until you are ready to froth milk for cappuccino or steam milk for lattes. The pump does not operate in the steam mode on a pump-boiler system.

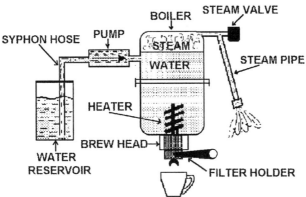

Steam is not generated unless there is water in the boiler, and the amount of steam generated at one time is related to the size of the boiler. Brewing espresso draws water from the reservoir into the boiler. If you are generating a great deal of steam without brewing espresso, the boiler may need refilling.

To refill the boiler at any time, activate the Coffee Switch to On, and the pump will refill the boiler. This is the same as priming the machine detailed in the section "Preparing Espresso".

Returning to the brewing mode after steaming requires a variable dwell time to lower the high-heat setting back to the brewing temperature.

PUMP THERMAL BLOCK SYSTEM

This is a relatively new innovation, similar in operation to the pump-boiler system, with the boiler replaced by a thermal block that contains the heating element. The thermal block resembles a radiator-like device with thin coiled channels that flash heat the water to the correct brewing or steaming temperatures.

In the brewing mode, water is pumped from the water reservoir into the thermal block where it is flash-heated to below boiling from 192-197°F. A status or ready light indicates when the water has reached the correct brewing temperature, and a thermostat maintains this temperature until you are ready to brew espresso.

When the steam switch is activated, the heating element switches to a high-heat setting to superheat the thermal block to the proper temperature for generating steam, 250-270°F. A ready light should indicate when the high-heat setting for steam has been reached. A second thermostat maintains this higher temperature until you are ready to froth or steam milk.

Steam is not released through the steam pipe until the steam valve (knob or lever) is opened and activates the pump. The pump operates in the steam mode in a thermal block system, drawing water from the reservoir and pulsing the water through the thermal block where it is flash-heated to generate steam. Steam is continuous in a thermal block system as long as there is water in the reservoir. You can tell if your system is a pump thermal block by the pulsing of the pump in the steaming mode.

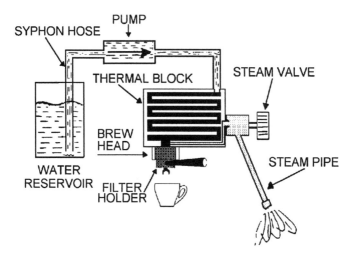

With both a pump-boiler and thermal block system, the ready light may cycle on and off in the brew mode or steam mode. This is normal and indicates the heating element is cycling to maintain the proper brewing or steaming temperatures.

However, not all machines have a ready light for the steam mode, and the time required to superheat the system must be estimated. If the system has not reached the optimum steaming temperature, the first burst of steam may be weak and watery.

To return to the brewing mode after steaming requires a dwell time to adjust the thermostat in the thermal block to the correct brewing temperature.

MACHINE CONTROLS & SWITCHES

OVERVIEW

A general overview of machine operation may make the entire brewing, steaming and frothing processes less intimidating and the results more rewarding. Most pump-driven espresso machines for home use are referred to as a "three switch, steam valve" machine. The three switches are:

1. Power On/Off Switch
2. Coffee On/Off Switch
3. Steam On/Off Switch

Steam Valve:

Either a knob or lever, the Steam Valve may be located on the right, left, or center of your espresso machine. The Steam Valve only releases steam through the steam pipe when the Valve is opened. The Steam On/Off Switch activates the high-heat setting in the boiler or thermal block, and the Steam Valve releases the steam. With the Coffee Switch On and the Steam Valve open, hot water is released through the steam pipe.

Important: Please refer to your owners manual to identify the location of these three switches and the Steam Valve on your particular machine.

Regardless of their position or configuration on the machine, these three switches and Steam Valve perform the following basic functions.

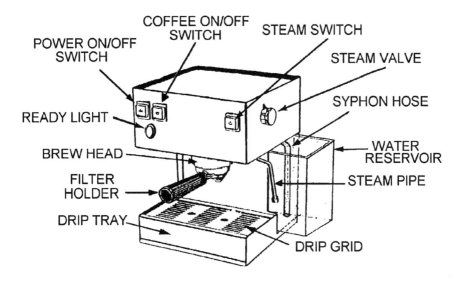

Power On/Off Switch:

This is the main power switch that activates the electrical components of the machine. The Power On/Off Switch also activates the heating element in the boiler or thermal block. Most machines have a Power On/Off indicator light built into the switch, or a separate light above or below the power switch.

Coffee On/Off Switch:

This switch is also referred to as the "pump" switch since the Coffee On/Off activates the pump and pumps water from the reservoir into the boiler or thermal block. The Coffee Switch will pump water through the system on demand, even though the water in the thermal block or boiler has not reached the correct brewing temperature.

The water (heated or unheated) is forced under pump pressure through the brew head. If you activate the Coffee On/Off Switch and open the Steam Valve, hot water will be directed to the steam pipe for either preparing hot tea or pre-heating espresso cups.

Steam Switch:

The sole purpose of this switch is to activate the high-heat thermostat and increase the temperature in the boiler or thermal block to generate steam. Steam is not released through the steam pipe until the Steam Valve is opened. A thermostat maintains the high heat setting for producing steam until the Steam Switch is returned to the Off position.

Ready (Status) Lights:

Most pump-driven espresso machines for home use have one or more ready lights that indicate the status of the temperatures in both the brewing and steaming modes. Some ready lights turn red, which indicate a "wait" condition while the temperature is converting, and the red light goes out when the brewing or steam temperature is reached. However, some ready lights turn green to indicate a "go" position, and the green light will illuminate when the correct temperature has been reached for brewing or steaming.

In the coffee mode, a ready light should indicate when the thermostat has reached the proper temperature below boiling for brewing espresso (from 192-197°F). In the steam mode, the ready light should indicate when the thermostat has superheated the water in the boiler or thermal block to generate steam (from 250-270°F).

Not all machines have ready lights to indicate the status, and the dwell time, or period of time it takes to convert the temperatures, must be estimated.

Steam Valve:

This valve is similar to a faucet, and, when opened with the Steam Switch On, the Steam Valve releases the steam that has accumulated at the top of the boiler or generated in the thermal block through the steam pipe. When the Coffee Switch is On and the Steam Valve is opened, hot water is directed to the steam pipe at approximately 197°F.

On a pump thermal block machine, the Steam Valve activates the pump that pulses water through the channels of the thermal block which flash-heat the water and generate steam through the steam pipe. If you hear and feel the pump pulsing in the steam mode, your machine is a thermal block system. With a pump-boiler system, the pump does not operate in the steam mode, and the Steam Valve releases the steam that has accumulated in the boiler.

IMPORTANT POINTS TO NOTE:

1. Be sure all switches of your machine are in the Off position before connecting the power cord to a 110-volt receptacle.

2. Since most espresso machines consume from 950 to 1500 watts of electrical power, it is important that your circuit is not overloaded with other appliances.

3. Do not turn On the Power Switch until you have read your instruction manual and you are ready to prime or ventilate the system. This is especially important on a new pump-boiler machine, since you want to avoid activating the heating element in the boiler before you have had an opportunity to fill the boiler with water by priming the system.

Do not confuse a full water reservoir with a full boiler. The water reservoir merely supplies fresh cold water to the system. The boiler is a separate vessel that contains the heating element, and water must be pumped from the water reservoir into the boiler inside the machine. Please refer to Chapter 6 "Priming the System".

4. Again, we emphasize that the information in this book IS NOT intended to supersede the information in the instruction manual supplied by the manufacturer of your espresso machine. Please refer to your instruction manual for specific information regarding the operation of your particular machine.

ANATOMY OF AN ESPRESSO MACHINE
PUMP THERMAL BLOCK

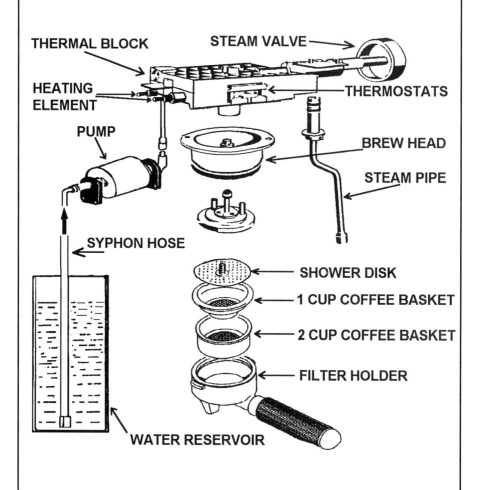

THERMAL BLOCK

STEAM VALVE

HEATING ELEMENT

THERMOSTATS

PUMP

BREW HEAD

STEAM PIPE

SYPHON HOSE

SHOWER DISK

1 CUP COFFEE BASKET

2 CUP COFFEE BASKET

FILTER HOLDER

WATER RESERVOIR

ANATOMY OF AN ESPRESSO MACHINE
PUMP BOILER

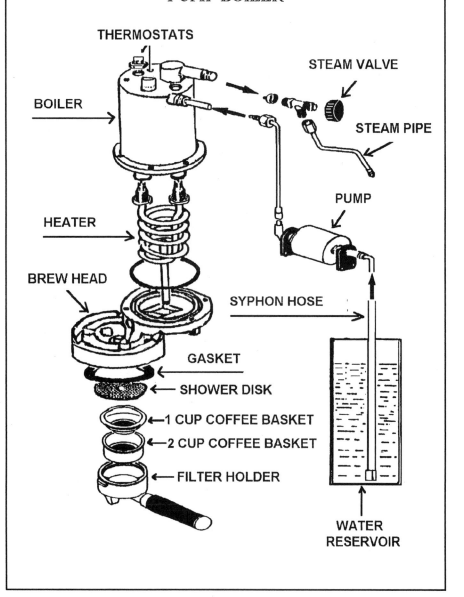

THERMOSTATS

STEAM VALVE

BOILER

STEAM PIPE

HEATER

PUMP

BREW HEAD

SYPHON HOSE

GASKET

SHOWER DISK

1 CUP COFFEE BASKET

2 CUP COFFEE BASKET

FILTER HOLDER

WATER
RESERVOIR

PREPARING CAFE-QUALITY ESPRESSO AT HOME

PREPARING CAFE-QUALITY ESPRESSO AT HOME

OVERVIEW

Even purchasing the most expensive espresso machine in the world is no assurance that you will brew a serving of café-quality espresso with crema. Extracting espresso with crema is akin to making a perfect soufflé. If you deviate even slightly from the basic rules and a tested recipe, your soufflé (or your espresso) can be disappointing.

One important factor often overlooked is the hygiene of the machine (covered in Chapter 9 under "Care and Maintenance"). A clean machine will help extract consistent servings of espresso with crema.

Special attention should be paid to pre-heating the machine and filter holder, because heat is a vital factor in preserving the flavor extraction in the small (1-1/2 to 2-ounce) espresso servings. The correct espresso grind is another crucial step, and grinding espresso coffee is covered both in this section and Chapter 3, "Coffee Grinders," and Chapter 4, "Espresso From Beans to Brew."

It is very important that the hot water under pressure flows evenly through the brew head and filter holder to completely saturate the finely ground coffee. Overextracting espresso, by allowing too much water to flow through the espresso grind, is a common mistake.

Do not be tempted to expose the finely ground coffee in the filter holder to the heated water for too much time. Some Baristas time the extraction from 15 to 20 seconds for a single serving of espresso. Others watch the change in color of the coffee as it lightens to a golden crema trickling from the filter holder into the cup.

PRIMING THE SYSTEM

Priming, also referred to as ventilating, means flushing or running fresh water through the espresso system to prime the pump and fill the boiler or induce water into the thermal block. This procedure will also eliminate any air pockets that may have developed in the system.

An air pocket in a new machine will "bounce" back and forth with the pulsing pump pressure and restrict the flow of water through the system. Priming a new system through the steam pipe will relieve any air pockets from the system. It is recommended that the system be primed through both the brew head and the steam pipe. Priming through the brew head with the filter holder in place (without coffee) not only pre-heats the system but also the filter holder to retain heat.

Priming through the brew head also flushes out any coffee residue that may have accumulated on the shower disk. Priming through the steam pipe flushes out milk that may have been drawn up into the steam pipe in addition to eliminating air pockets.

Use water liberally in the priming mode to keep your machine in top operating condition. Please refer to your instruction manual for specific instructions from the manufacturer for priming or ventilating your machine.

Important: Do not activate the Power Switch to On until you are ready to prime your system. Water should always be induced into the boiler of a pump-boiler system to avoid triggering a thermal cut-off as a result of heating an empty boiler. This is not critical with a pump thermal block system.

PRIMING THROUGH THE STEAM PIPE

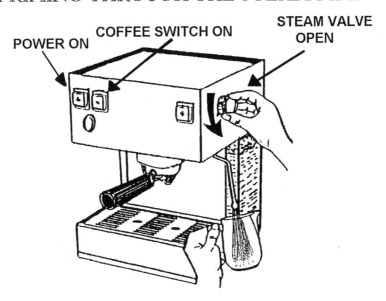

Most manufacturers recommend that you place a pitcher under the steam pipe, open the Steam Valve, activate the Power Switch to On, and depress the Coffee Switch to On.

This will activate the pump to begin priming hot water through the steam pipe. With a brand new machine, you should prime a considerable amount of water (several cups) through the system to evacuate any industrial residue which may be left over from the manufacturing process.

If an air pocket develops in the system, the only way to eliminate the air pocket in a boiler or thermal block is to prime the system through the steam pipe.

PRIMING THROUGH THE BREW HEAD

Priming through the brew head is recommended for flushing the shower disk of coffee residue and pre-heating the filter holder (without coffee in the coffee basket). Place a cup beneath the brew head, with or without the filter holder in place.

**POWER
ON**   **COFFEE
ON**   **STEAM
OFF**

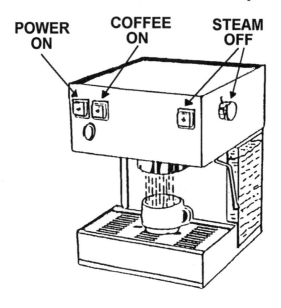

Turn the Power Switch On and activate the Coffee Switch to On. This will energize the pump to draw water from the water reservoir into the boiler or thermal block. It will take from 15 to 20 seconds for water to flow through the brew head.

After 60 seconds, if water does not begin to flow, turn the Coffee Switch Off to stop the pumping action. More than 60 seconds to generate a flow of water through the brew head may indicate an air pocket that prevents the pump from priming properly. At this point, you should prime your system through the steam pipe as outlined on page 87.

Priming through the brew head is an important maintenance function, since it prevents the build up of coffee residue.

ESPRESSO WITH CREMA
STEP-BY-STEP

The following steps assume that your machine has been properly primed and the water reservoir is filled with fresh cold water. Also make sure the siphon hose is immersed in the water supply (not all machines have a siphon hose).

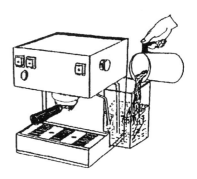

Activate the Power Switch to On. The heating element will begin heating the water in the boiler or thermal block.

Wait until the ready light signals that the water has reached the correct brewing temperature. Some machines have a ready light that goes on (usually green), while others have a ready light that goes out (usually red), when the thermostat has reached the brewing temperature from 192°F to 197°F.

POWER ON **READY LIGHT ON**

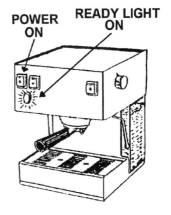

We recommend that you allow your machine to fully pre-heat, with the filter holder in the brew head, for at least five minutes before brewing your first serving of espresso.

Insert either the one or two-cup coffee basket into the filter holder. We recommend using the one-cup coffee basket for your trial and error sessions.

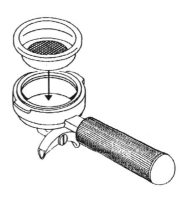

Fill the coffee basket with finely ground espresso coffee, about two tablespoons (approximately 7 grams per serving). Double this amount for the two-cup coffee basket. Do not overfill the coffee basket or the filter holder may not lock into the brew head.

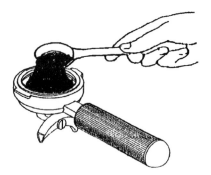

Lightly tap the side of the filter holder with the tamper to evenly distribute the coffee in the coffee basket. Tamp the coffee by firmly depressing the tamper on top of the finely ground coffee, with a slight twist of the tamper to polish the surface.

Wipe the edge of the filter holder with your palm or finger to remove any grounds that may affect the seal between the filter holder and brew head.

Pressurized water will follow the path of least resistance through the coffee grind, which is why the tamping process is important for the full extraction of the espresso flavor.

The purpose of tamping is to level the grind in the coffee basket to ensure complete saturation of the ground coffee. In addition, the compressed grind provides resistance in the brew head, which creates additional pressure for maximum flavor extraction.

If your coffee is ground too coarse,
heavier tamping may help correct
the problem. However, firmly
tamping a grind that is too fine may
completely block the flow of water
through the brew head.

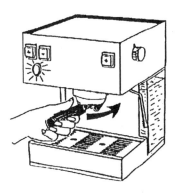

Place the filter holder into the brew
head, turn (usually from left to right)
and lock in place in accordance with
the manufacturer's instructions.
Until you get the feel for this locking
action, visually inspect the filter
holder to be sure it is seated properly
in the brew head to avoid splattering
hot coffee.

Place one or two pre-heated
espresso cups under the filter holder
spigots. If you are brewing a single
serving of espresso, center the cup
under the two spigots and, for two
servings, place two cups side by side
directly beneath each spigot.

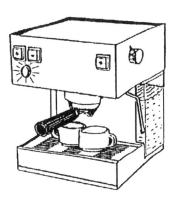

Activate the Coffee Switch to On.
You should now hear the pump
operating, which may be somewhat
noisy depending on your machine.

COFFEE
OFF

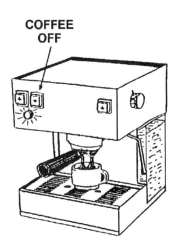

It will take 15 to 20 seconds for the
water to build up pressure in the
brew head. You should then see a
trickle of golden brown espresso
ooze into the cup(s).

It should take only 20 to 30 seconds
to extract 1-1/2 ounces of espresso
for a single serving, and slightly longer
for double servings.

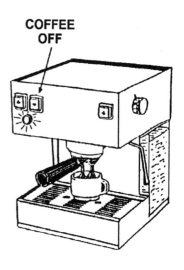

**COFFEE
OFF**

Turn Off the Coffee Switch as soon
as you have extracted 1-1/2 ounces
per serving.

Remove the filter holder from the
brew head, and tap out the used coffee
grounds in a grounds tray or waste
bin. (If you tap your filter holder
against the side of a garbage basket,
be sure you are not depositing the
coffee basket from the filter holder in the garbage. This seems to
be a rather common occurrence based on the number of people
that order replacement coffee baskets.)

Wipe the bottom of the brew head and shower disk with a damp
cloth to remove any coffee residue. Priming through the brew
head will also flush any residue that may have accumulated on top
of the shower disk.

Why brew only 1½ ounces if you
do not like "strong" espresso? If
you allow more than 1½ ounces of
water to flow through a one-cup
coffee basket, you will begin
extracting some of the bitter oils
from the grounds. Overextraction
defeats the purpose of espresso.

**2 1/2 OUNCE
ESPRESSO CUP**

It should be noted that the size of the espresso serving is related
to the size of the coffee basket and filter holder. A larger one-cup
coffee basket will allow an extraction of two full ounces without
overextracting the espresso.

You want to quickly extract only the heart and essence of the coffee flavor. If you prefer your espresso lighter, dilute the serving with hot water from the steam pipe to create "espresso lungo", or consider one of the lighter variations listed under "Recipes".

At this point, you are either elated or disappointed with your espresso serving. If you were fortunate, you brewed a perfect cup of espresso with the elusive crema on top. Congratulations! You are one of few to do so on the first attempt.

If you were not so fortunate, outlined on the following page are some reasons why your first attempt fell short of the perfect cup.

As we have emphasized throughout this book, producing a perfect espresso with crema is a rather complex endeavor that takes a great deal of trial, error, and patience to fine-tune your skills. But the reward is well worth the effort.

The first time you extract espresso with the creamy, golden crema, you will enjoy the delightful flavor of true espresso, the most popular beverage in the world.

WHAT WENT WRONG?

Espresso does not flow out of the filter holder:
* No water in the water reservoir
* Siphon hose not inserted in the reservoir
* Coffee ground too fine or tamped too hard
* Too much coffee in the coffee basket
* An air pocket is in the system

Espresso flows too quickly:
* Coffee ground too coarse
* Not enough coffee or not tamped
* Water had not reached the correct brewing temperature

Espresso spurts from around the filter holder:
* Filter holder not seated properly in brew head
* Coffee grounds around the filter holder rim
* Too much coffee in the coffee basket
* Coffee ground too fine or tamped too hard
* Brew head gasket needs cleaning or replacing

Espresso has a bitter taste, no Crema:
* Coffee not fresh
* Grind needs adjustment
* System not pre-heated
* Coffee overextracted
* Shower disk needs cleaning

Espresso has scalded or burnt taste:
* Steam was produced first, and the temperature was
  not allowed to drop to the correct brewing temperature

Espresso not hot enough:
* Water did not reach the correct brewing temperature
* Filter holder, brew head and cups were not pre-heated

FROTHING AND STEAMING MILK

FROTHING AND STEAMING MILK

OVERVIEW

This chapter of our book should be of particular interest because milk-based espresso beverages are far more popular in North America than straight espresso. The estimated percentage of straight espresso served in North America is only 10% to 15% of all espresso-related beverages, and this varies by region. The remaining 85% or 90% is an endless variety of milk-based drinks such as, cappuccino, caffè latte, flavored lattes, steamers, mochas, breves, and iced espresso drinks.

Lattes are currently out-selling cappuccino in North America. By contrast, straight espresso is the traditional after-lunch and after-dinner drink in Italy and other Southern European countries. Experts claim the reason for the overwhelming popularity of milk-based espresso drinks in North America is due to improperly brewed espresso commonly served here, which has a rather unpleasant taste. They claim the addition of a hot milk or flavored additive covers the espresso's deficiency, and a true espresso with crema should be savored straight.

In Europe, milk-based espresso drinks are rarely consumed after breakfast. Europeans usually serve steamed (not frothed) milk with their espresso as a breakfast drink, called Caffè Latte in Italian, Café au Lait in French, Café con Leche in Spanish, and Kaffe mit Milch in German.

Milk-based espresso drinks fall into two categories: those that use a combination of steamed and frothed milk for cappuccino-type drinks; and steamed milk only, for drinks like caffè latte and flavored steamers without espresso.

To understand the difference between frothed and steamed milk, when you follow the instructions for frothing milk for cappuccino, you will note the bottom half of the pitcher has steamed milk (without bubbles) and the top half is frothed milk that has been highly aerated with small bubbles that form a foam or froth. Frothed milk is thicker in consistency than steamed milk.

Cappuccino derives its name from the order of Capuchin monks, recognized in Italy by their brown hooded robes, who originally developed this delicious combination of espresso with steamed and frothed milk. The frothed milk from the top of the steaming pitcher is spooned on top to "cap" the cappuccino and retain heat.

There are many variables in the art of frothing milk, and each machine seems to have its own characteristics. Although we are outlining the basic steps most commonly used, again, trial and error will prevail. After you have some practice, slight variations to these basic procedures may help you to achieve consistent results.

Don't get discouraged. We have known many that practiced for several weeks before they were able to master the techniques of steaming milk without scalding and perfecting their froth.

FROTHING MILK FOR CAPPUCCINO STEP-BY-STEP

With the Power Switch On, the water reservoir full, and the machine primed, activate the Steam Switch to On. The thermostat in the heating element switches to the high-heat setting, (250°F to 270°F) to super-heat the boiler or thermal block for generating steam.

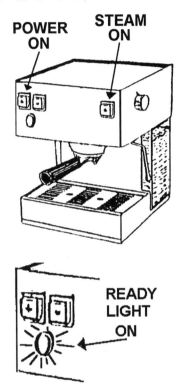

POWER ON   STEAM ON

It will take from 30 to 60 seconds (depending on the machine) to convert the temperature from below 198°F to the high heat for steam. This conversion or recovery period is called the "dwell time". On most machines a ready light will indicate when the water in the boiler or thermal block has reached the proper temperature for steam. A thermostat maintains this high-heat level until the Steam Switch is turned Off.

READY LIGHT ON

Place an empty cup or pitcher under the steam pipe, and open the Steam Valve for several seconds. This will clear any condensation or moisture that has accumulated in the steam pipe. Close the Steam Valve.

This not only prevents diluting the milk but, in a pump-boiler system, also creates more space in the top of the boiler for the expansion of steam.

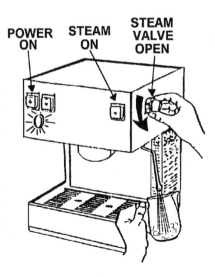

POWER ON   STEAM ON   STEAM VALVE OPEN

Now you are ready to froth milk.

Fill a pitcher 1/3 full of fresh, cold milk, the colder the better. Non-fat or 2% milk is easier to froth. Whole milk, although slightly more difficult to froth, produces a denser, creamier froth. Warm or old milk will not froth. A chilled frothing pitcher greatly assists in the frothing process. A stainless steel pitcher will chill in the freezer in five minutes.

Place the tip of the steam pipe just below (1/2" below) the surface of the milk, and fully open the Steam Valve to release the steam into the frothing pitcher. Move the pitcher slowly in either a circular or up and down motion.

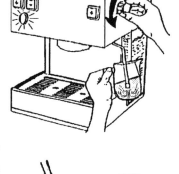

As the milk expands in volume, very slowly lower the pitcher, keeping the steam pipe just below the surface of the milk to blend the froth thoroughly and eliminate big bubbles.

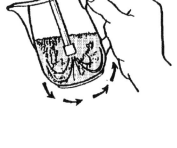

Eventually you will identify the sound with the frothing process. A high-pitched screeching or howling noise indicates the milk is scalding, while aerating the milk sounds like a low, muffled rumbling noise.

Many Baristas rely on a thermometer clipped onto the frothing pitcher to make sure that the temperature does not reach the scalding point of 150°F. But even they still gauge the frothing process by sound.

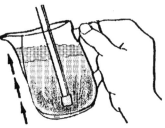

After the volume of milk in the pitcher doubles or triples, if necessary, you may further heat the milk by raising the pitcher and lowering the steam pipe to the bottom of the pitcher. This is a critical point in the frothing process. Be careful not to scald the milk, which will dissipate the froth. The milk temperature for frothing should range between 135°F and 150°F.

Turn the Steam Valve Off before removing the steam pipe from the pitcher to avoid splattering hot milk. Tap the pitcher on the counter lightly, and set it aside to settle the frothed milk on top of the steamed milk in the pitcher.

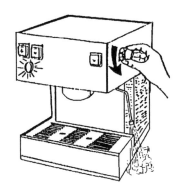

Open the Steam Valve for a short (two second) burst of steam to evacuate any milk that may have been drawn up into the steam pipe. This is an important procedure, since, not only will hardened milk clog the steam pipe and eventually inhibit the flow of steam, but milk can also be drawn up through the steam pipe into the boiler or thermal block which can contaminate the water supply.

Always wipe the steam pipe with a wet cloth to remove the milk coating before it hardens. Hardened milk can be difficult to remove once it has solidified on the steam pipe.

5 OUNCE CAPPUCCINO CUP

Ideally, the frothed milk in the top half of the pitcher will be smooth and thick, and the froth should not dissipate quickly. A good froth consists of small bubbles and has a creamy texture. Underneath the froth you will have steamed milk.

Each espresso machine seems to have its own frothing idiosyncrasies, and, therefore, the question of rotating the pitcher as opposed to using an up and down motion somewhat depends on the characteristics of your machine.

It may take a good deal of practice to develop your best frothing technique. The type of milk used will greatly affect the frothing process. Whole milk will develop a froth with more body, but low fat milk is easier to froth. Half-and-half or cream are not recommended because of the high butter fat content that make them difficult to froth.

The object is to froth long enough to form small, tight bubbles in the milk, but not too long or the milk will scald and quickly dissipate any froth and impart a burnt taste to the milk.

Many machines now feature an aerator attached to the steam pipe to induce more air into the milk and enhance the frothing process. However, some aerators tend to create large bubbles that are impressive at first but dissipate quickly.

The proportion of espresso to steamed and frothed milk for cappuccino is usually 1/3 espresso, 1/3 steamed milk and 1/3 frothed milk on top to "cap" the cappuccino and retain the heat. If you prefer a stronger coffee flavor, you may always alter the proportions to 1/2 espresso, 1/4 steamed milk and 1/4 frothed milk. Or, prepare a "dry" cappuccino with one shot of espresso and all frothed milk.

Some prefer to pour the espresso from a separate cup over the steamed and frothed milk in a five-ounce cappuccino cup. The espresso "marks" the white froth. Others pour the steamed milk into an espresso serving in the cappuccino cup and spoon the frothed milk on top. Experiment with both methods to determine your preference.

If your early frothing results are disappointing, don't despair. It usually takes a great deal of practice to produce a smooth, thick froth. And, with practice, you will define your own recipe for success.

STEAMING MILK FOR CAFFE LATTE

The literal translation of the Italian caffè latte is coffee with milk. Europeans usually prepare their morning coffee by pouring espresso and steamed milk together into a nine to 12-ounce breakfast cup, varying the proportions based on personal taste. A traditional Swiss breakfast drink includes cubes of dried bread to make a type of porridge.

Caffè latte was first popularized in North America in the Pacific Northwest, mainly Seattle, usually prepared with a slight variation to the European recipe. Most lattes served here include a dollop of frothed milk layered on top. A classic caffè latte is roughly 1/3 espresso with 2/3 steamed milk.

Steam is the clear vapor between hot water and a visible mist. Milk heated with live steam has a much better taste than milk heated in a saucepan over a burner on the stove. Heating milk with live steam alters the proteins of the milk and changes the texture for an improved taste.

Not all drinks need espresso. Even a classic hot chocolate tastes better using milk heated with live steam. Steamers are made by steaming flavored milk without espresso. Steaming would also seem like a logical way to heat the baby's formula and make an early convert to the espresso craze.

BASIC CAFFE LATTE AMERICAN-STYLE

1. Prepare a single serving of espresso in a five-ounce cup, or a double serving in a nine-ounce pre-heated cup.

2. Activate the Steam On/Off Switch to begin super heating the water in the boiler or the thermal block.

3. Fill your frothing pitcher from one-third to half full of fresh, cold milk (lattes use more milk than frothing for cappuccino).

4. When the steam ready light indicates the proper steaming temperature has been reached, open the Steam Valve for a few seconds, then turn Off the Steam Valve. This will evacuate excess moisture from the steam pipe and avoid diluting the milk.

5. Place the steam pipe below the surface of the milk in the pitcher and open the Steam Valve.

6. Slowly rotate the pitcher and, as the milk thickens, raise the pitcher and lower the steam pipe deeper into the milk. Be careful not to scald the milk which will impart a burnt taste. The temperature of the milk should not exceed 150°F.

7. Turn off the Steam Valve before removing the steam pipe from the steaming pitcher, then remove the pitcher from the steam pipe.

8. Open the Steam Valve for a few seconds to evacuate any milk that may have been drawn up into the steam pipe, and wipe the steam pipe with a damp cloth to remove any milk coating that may harden later.

10. Holding back the slight froth at the top of the pitcher with a spoon, pour the steamed milk into the espresso serving to fill the cup. Spoon on a "cap" of froth to retain the heat of your caffè latte.

There is a fine line between a cappuccino and a caffè latte, usually related to the size of the serving and proportion of froth to steamed milk. Cappuccino is usually served in a five-ounce cup or glass with equal thirds of espresso, steamed milk, and frothed milk. A caffè latte has more than half steamed milk and is usually served in a larger cup with a capacity from nine to 12 ounces.

Another version of an expanded cappuccino is the "latteccino" with more frothed milk added to the latte. Flavored lattes and steamers are gaining in popularity. Flavorings dissolve better when added to the cup before the espresso, or blended with milk when steaming.

Please refer to the Recipe section and the charts listing flavored syrups and garnishes to complete your home "espresso bar." Milk-based beverages offer endless possibilities, including substituting soy milk for those allergic to milk, and steamers for those that have not yet acquired the taste for espresso.

SUMMARY

CAPPUCCINO & LATTES

1. Always start with fresh, cold milk, the colder the better

2. Turn the Steam Switch On to activate the high-heat setting

3. Wait for the Ready Light to indicate the correct steaming temperature has been reached

4. Briefly open the Steam Valve to purge any moisture from the steam pipe

5. Insert the steam pipe below the surface of the milk before opening the Steam Valve

6. A high-pitched screeching sound indicates the milk is scalding, which ruins the froth and gives the milk a burnt taste

7. Turn off the Steam Valve before removing the pitcher from the steam pipe to avoid splattering hot milk

8. Open the Steam Valve for a short burst to evacuate any milk that may have been drawn into the steam pipe

9. Wipe the steam pipe with a wet cloth to remove the milk coating before it hardens

10. Turn off the Steam Switch to return to the brewing mode

CHAPTER 8

RECIPES
CLASSIC
&
CONTEMPORARY

CLASSIC &
CONTEMPORARY
RECIPES

With the basic elements already detailed for preparing espresso with crema, frothy cappuccino and smooth caffè latte, the pleasure in enjoying your espresso equipment really begins. Having mastered the brewing, frothing and steaming techniques, an endless variety of beverages await you.

The following pages are divided between classic and contemporary recipes for the three basic categories; espresso, cappuccino and latte. Also included are recipes for mochas, iced beverages, and espresso drinks with spirits, along with charts on flavorings, garnishes, liqueurs and accessories to complete your home espresso bar.

Latte Lingo

The social culture surrounding espresso has created a language all its own. In Italy, if you order just a "latte" you will be served a glass of milk. Ordering just a "latte" in North America now includes a long list of variations we are calling "latte lingo".

Latte	Standard latte in an 8-ounce cup
Short	Small latte in a 5-ounce cup
Tall	Large latte in a 12-ounce cup
Grande	Extra large in a 16-ounce cup
Double Short	Double shot of espresso in a 5-ounce cup
Double Tall	Double shot of espresso in a 12-ounce cup
Tall Skinny	Large latte made with non-fat milk
Tall Two	Large latte made with 2% milk
Harmless	Latte using decaffeinated espresso
Skinny Sleeper	Latte with decaf and non-fat milk
Foamless	Latte with steamed milk, no froth
Steamer	Flavored latte without espresso
Breve	Latte with Half-n-Half instead of milk
Wet	Cappuccino with steamed and frothed milk
Dry	Cappuccino with frothed milk only
Americano	Espresso diluted with hot water

The list goes on, and everyone can join the fun; from steamers for kids, to skinnies for calorie counters. After experimenting with the following recipes, you may find yourself using the same lingo to describe your own signature drinks.

Classic Espresso Recipes

Espresso

A single serving of espresso, roughly 1-1/2 ounces, served in a 2-1/2 ounce, pre-heated demi-tasse cup.

Espresso Ristretto

A short or "restricted" espresso, where the flow of water through the brew head is stopped at about 1 ounce per serving.

Espresso Lungo

A single serving of espresso diluted with hot water to produce a milder or "long" espresso. Also called an "Americano" the espresso is diluted with hot water from the steam pipe, not from the brew head, to resemble American drip coffee but with a richer espresso flavor.

Espresso Doppio

A double serving of espresso, from three to four ounces. Use the two-cup coffee basket in the filter holder and serve in a five-ounce cappuccino cup.

Espresso Macchiato

A single serving of espresso "marked" with one or two tablespoons of frothed milk.

Espresso con Panna

A single or double espresso serving topped with whipped cream. Serve the single in a demi-tasse cup and the double serving in a five-ounce cappuccino cup, and garnish with chocolate.

Espresso Romano

A single serving of espresso served with a fresh lemon peel. The lemon peel should be served only on the saucer, not in the espresso, since the citrus acid will dissipate any crema.

Legend indicates the lemon peel was originally served with espresso to sanitize the cup rim, and using the lemon peel after drinking espresso also cleaned one's teeth. Another version claims that after WWII the coffee available in Europe was of such poor quality that the lemon peel was used to alter the coffee flavor. This is not an Italian custom today, but Espresso Romano is often served in restaurants in North America.

Espresso Sugars

Flavored sugar is an elegant way to sweeten espresso. Sprinkle one cup of sugar with one teaspoon of grated lemon or orange rind and mix well. Or, bury two whole vanilla beans in one pound of granulated sugar. Cinnamon, nutmeg and cloves can also be used for flavoring. Store flavored espresso sugar in an air-tight container in the refrigerator.

Contemporary Espresso Recipes

Caffè Borgia

Add one espresso serving to 3/4 ounce of Creme de Cacao syrup (non-alcoholic) in a five-ounce cappuccino cup. Top with whipped cream and garnish with nutmeg.

Espresso au Miel (honey)

Cover the bottom of a demi-tasse cup with honey, and brew a single serving of espresso directly into the cup. Blend well and sweeten with sugar to taste.

Espresso Mandarin

Add a double (doppio) serving of espresso to 1/4 or 1/2 ounce of orange (Mandarino) syrup and garnish with an orange slice.

Spiced Apple Americano

Pour 1/2 ounce apple syrup and 1/4 ounce cinnamon syrup into a 12-ounce latte cup or glass. Prepare an Espresso Lungo (Americano) by combining 5 ounces of hot water (from the steam pipe) with a double (doppio) serving of espresso, and add to the syrups in the latte cup. Adjust the amount of hot water and syrup to taste. Garnish with a cinnamon stick for stirring.

Classic Cappuccino Recipes

The proportion of steamed and frothed milk varies according to taste. These recipes are based on a single serving of espresso brewed into a pre-heated five-ounce cappuccino cup. For a double cappuccino, prepare an espresso doppio (three to four ounces), double the amount of steamed and frothed milk, and serve in a larger nine to 12-ounce latte cup or glass.

Cappuccino

Traditionally cappuccino is 1/3 espresso, 1/3 steamed milk, and 1/3 frothed milk served in a five-ounce, pre-heated cappuccino cup. Cappuccino is topped with foam by spooning the frothed milk on top of the serving. Although it is not a European tradition, cappuccino can be garnished with a light sprinkle of chocolate or cocoa, cinnamon, nutmeg or vanilla powder.

Dry Cappuccino

Served in a five-ounce pre-heated cappuccino cup, the proportion is 1/3 espresso to 2/3 frothed milk, without steamed milk, also lightly garnished with a sprinkle of chocolate, cinnamon, nutmeg or vanilla powder.

Mocha

A cappuccino with chocolate, the Mocha is a mixture of 1/3 espresso and 2/3 frothed and steamed milk where chocolate has been dissolved, served in a five-ounce cappuccino cup or glass. Powdered cocoa or chocolate syrup are stirred into the milk before frothing, adjusting the proportions according to taste.

Michael's Cappuccino

Whisk one egg white with 1/4 teaspoon vanilla extract until it forms soft peaks. Spoon two heaping teaspoons of this mixture into a five-ounce pre-heated cappuccino cup or glass. Brew a two ounce serving of espresso into the cup and top with frothed milk.

Contemporary Cappuccino Recipes

Creamy Coconut Cappuccino

Pour 1/2 ounce coconut syrup and 1/2 ounce vanilla syrup into a five-ounce cappuccino cup. Add espresso, stir, and add steamed milk. Top with frothed milk and garnish with a sprinkle of chocolate.

Hazelnut Cappuccino

Pour 1/2 ounce hazelnut syrup into a five-ounce cappuccino cup. Add espresso, stir, and add steamed milk. Top with frothed milk and garnish with vanilla powder.

Peach Spice Cappuccino

Pour 1/2 ounce peach syrup and 1/4 ounce cinnamon syrup. Prepare a cappuccino, adding the espresso to the syrups first, then the steamed milk and top with 1/3 frothed milk. Garnish with ground cinnamon.

Peanut Butter Mocha

Add 1 tablespoon smooth peanut butter to a thick chocolate syrup and blend well. Add espresso and stir. Froth milk in a steaming pitcher and, holding back the froth with a spoon, pour steamed milk into the espresso mixture. Top with a 2" layer of frothed milk and garnish with chocolate sprinkles.

Raspberry Banana Cappuccino

Pour 1/2 ounce raspberry syrup and 1/4 ounce banana syrup into a five-ounce cappuccino cup. Add espresso, stir, and add steamed milk. Top with frothed milk and garnish with vanilla powder.

Vanilla Cappuccino

Pour 3/4 ounce vanilla syrup in a steaming pitcher and fill 1/3 full with fresh, cold milk. Froth the vanilla and milk mixture. Add the steamed milk to an espresso serving in a pre-heated five-ounce cappuccino cup. Top with frothed milk and sprinkle with cocoa.

Classic Caffè Latte Recipes

Caffè Latte

Known by the French as Café au Lait, the Italian Caffè Latte is usually 1/3 espresso to 2/3 steamed milk, or a three ounce double serving espresso to five ounces of steamed milk, served in a large nine-ounce, bowl-shaped cup or wide-mouthed glass.

Caffè Breve

A breve substitutes Half-n-Half for milk, prepared and served the same as a Caffè Latte. Remember that Half-n-Half or cream will not froth, but steaming Half-n-Half for Breves adds an even richer texture than steamed milk.

Latteccino

An Americanized Caffè Latte with frothed milk spooned on top of the espresso and steamed milk, a cross between a cappuccino and latte.

Latte Macchiato

A glass of steamed milk into which a single serving of espresso is slowly dribbled, to "mark" the milk with espresso.

Contemporary Latte Recipes

Blueberry Cream Breve

Combine 1/2 ounce blueberry syrup and 1/2 ounce vanilla syrup. Prepare a Caffè Latte substituting Half-n-Half for milk. Add the espresso then the steamed cream to the syrups and stir

Cherry Brandy Latte

Pour 1/2 ounce cherry syrup and 1/4 ounce Amaretto (non-alcoholic) syrup into a nine to 12-ounce latte cup. Prepare a Caffè Latte, adding first the espresso then the steamed milk to the combined syrups.

Cherry Breve

Pour one ounce of cherry syrup in a latte cup. Prepare an espresso (a single or double serving) and add to the cup. Steam Half-n-Half and fill the cup. Substituting steamed milk for Half-n-Half becomes a Cherry Latte.

Egg Nog Latte

Fill a pitcher 1/2 full of egg nog and steam. Fill a latte cup almost full with the steamed egg nog, and add espresso. Garnish with cinnamon and nutmeg.

French Vanilla Double Latte

Pour 1/2 ounce hazelnut syrup and one ounce vanilla syrup in a large 12-ounce breakfast cup or latte glass. Prepare a double espresso serving (three ounces) and add to the syrup mixture. Steam milk with a slight foam on top. Holding back the froth with a spoon, fill the cup with steamed milk and spoon a layer of frothed milk on top. Garnish with cocoa or chocolate sprinkles.

Fuzzy Navel

Pour one ounce peach syrup and 1/2 orange syrup in a 12 ounce latte cup. Prepare a Caffè Latte, pouring the espresso into the syrup mixture first, and filling the cup with steamed milk. Top with whipped cream, if desired, and garnish with cinnamon. Substitute steamed Half-n-Half for a Fuzzy Navel Breve.

Mint Mocha Latte

Pour 1/4 ounce crème de menthe syrup and 1/2 ounce chocolate syrup in a latte cup. Prepare a Caffè Latte, add the espresso to the syrups, and fill the cup with steamed milk. Substituting steamed Half-n-Half for steamed milk becomes a Mint Mocha Breve.

Mocha Nut Latte

Pour 1/4 ounce almond syrup, 1/4 ounce hazelnut syrup, and 1/2 ounce chocolate syrup in a latte cup. Prepare a Caffè Latte, adding the espresso to the syrup mixture first and fill the cup with steamed milk. Garnish with vanilla powder.

For the Pastry Chef:

Espresso Almond Bars:

2-1/4 cups flour	1 egg
1 cup sugar	1 Tbs. ground espresso
1 cup butter	1 cup sliced almonds

Preheat oven to 350°. Cream the butter and sugar, add the egg and ground espresso. Mix in flour, then almonds. Press the mixture into a pan 13" x 9" x 2" and bake 25-30 minutes, until the edges turn light brown. Cut into bars while slightly warm, and cool completely. Remove from pan and dust with powdered sugar.

Mocha Macaroons

2 ounces unsweetened chocolate	1 cup chopped nuts
one 14 ounce can sweetened	1-1/2 ounce espresso
condensed milk	1 teaspoon almond extract
2 cups finely shredded coconut	1/8 teaspoon salt

Preheat oven to 350°. In a large saucepan combine the chocolate and milk, and cook over medium heat stirring briskly with a whisk until thick and glossy. Remove from the heat and add remaining ingredients, and blend well. Drop small teaspoonfuls of the chocolate mixture one inch apart on a greased baking sheet. Bake 10 minutes or until the bottoms are set, but do not overbake. The macaroons should have a soft, chewy texture. Transfer to waxed paper to cool.

Tiramisu

A classic Italian layered dessert, there are many variations to this recipe. This version uses a pound cake base which can be store-bought or made from scratch; other versions use Madeleine-type cookies (or Lady Fingers) as the base.

1 pound cake thinly sliced
2 cups espresso
2 tablespoons dark rum
6 large egg yolks
1/2 cup sugar

2 tablespoons flour
2 tablespoons Marsala wine
1 cup whipping cream
1 lb. Mascarpone cheese
6-8 ounces semisweet chocolate

Arrange a layer of loaf-shaped pound cake thinly sliced in the bottom of a 13" x 9" x 2" baking pan. Mix espresso with dark rum, and drizzle half over the cake slices. Whisk egg yolks, sugar and flour in a heavy saucepan. Cook over medium heat, stirring constantly, until the mixture thickens. Remove from the heat and add Marsala.

Whip cream with an electric mixer until it forms soft peaks, and transfer to a mixing bowl. Beat Mascarpone lightly, and add the egg yolk mixture. Blend until smooth, and fold in whipped cream. Spread half of this cheese mixture over the cake slices in the pan; top with remaining cake slices and drizzle remaining espresso mixture over the cake slices. Spread with remaining cheese and garnish with shaved chocolate. Refrigerate at least two hours before serving for best results.

Iced Espresso Beverages

Almost any hot version of espresso drinks can be served over ice. To preserve the espresso flavor when ice melts, consider freezing espresso ice cubes. Bear in mind that one melted ice cube is about two ounces of water, and espresso ice cubes will intensify the espresso flavor.

Granitas have become popular, which is an adaptation of an Italian dessert similar to a flavored sorbet. Commercial granita machines, keep ice and flavored syrups rotating at a controlled temperature to keep the ingredients from solidifying. You can prepare granitas at home using the blender, adapting most of the latte, mocha and breve recipes to crushed iced versions.

When preparing iced drinks in a tall glass or in the blender, add the flavored syrup first, then freshly brewed espresso, and stir to blend the flavors. Add cold milk (or Half-n-Half next), and ice last. Garnish after the beverage has been poured.

Espresso Granita

In a blender, combine 1/4 cup Amaretto syrup, 1/4 cup Kahlua syrup, 1-1/2 cups vanilla (or coffee) ice cream, and seven espresso ice cubes. Process until smooth and frothy.

Italian Sodas

Club soda and flavored syrups served over ice become a refreshing Italian Soda. Start with two ounces of any flavoring in an eight-ounce glass with ice, and fill with club soda. Begin combining flavorings and adjusting the proportions per serving to taste. The following are only a few of the many varieties awaiting your imagination.

Amaretto Cooler

Pour 1-1/2 ounce amaretto syrup and 1/2 ounce lemon syrup in a tall eight-ounce glass, and add ice. Fill with soda water and stir.

Blueberry Banana

Pour 1-1/2 ounce blueberry syrup and one ounce of banana syrup in a tall 12-ounce glass and add ice. Add one ounce of Half-n-Half and fill the glass with club soda.

Cranberry Soda

Pour one ounce cranberry syrup, 1/2 ounce lemon syrup and 1/2 ounce coconut syrup in an eight-ounce glass. Add ice and fill with club soda.

Cream Soda

Pour two ounces of vanilla syrup in an eight-ounce glass, add ice and fill with club soda.

Tropicana

Pour 1/2 ounce coconut syrup and 1/2 ounce pineapple syrup in a tall eight-ounce glass. Add a double serving of espresso and blend well. Pour in two ounces of cold Half-n-Half. Add ice and fill the glass with club soda.

Venetian Bellini

Pour 1-1/2 ounce peach syrup and 1/2 ounce apple syrup in an eight-ounce glass, and add ice. Fill with soda water and add a splash of lime syrup.

Flavored Syrups & Garnishes

A wide variety of flavored syrups are now available in fruit, nut, liqueur and chocolate flavors. Syrups should be poured into the cup before the espresso, or added to the milk before frothing or steaming. The quantity suggested to start is 1/4 to 1/2 ounce per flavor. This will vary by the size of the serving and personal taste. Be adventurous, just experiment and enjoy!

Fruit Flavored Syrups

Apple	Cranberry
Apricot	Grape
Banana	Lemon/Lime
Blackberry/Blueberry	Orange
Boysenberry	Peach
Butterscotch	Pineapple
Cherry	Raspberry/Strawberry

Nut Flavored Syrups

Almond	Hazelnut
Chocolate/Chocolate Mint	Honey
Cinnamon	Praline
Coconut	Vanilla

Non-Alcoholic Liqueur Flavored Syrups

Amaretto	Irish Creme
Creme de Cacao	Kahlua
Creme de Menthe	Rum

For the final embellishment of your beverage consider these toppings:

Garnishes & Toppings

Grated / Ground	Peel / Zest	Dairy-Based
Brown Sugar	Lemon	Frothed Milk
Chocolate	Lime	Half 'N Half
Cinnamon	Orange	Steamed Milk
Nutmeg		Whipped Cream
Vanilla		Whisked Egg Whites

Combining flavorings and garnishes for your signature drinks offers endless possibilities, and a true mixologist will experiment freely.

Espresso Drinks Fortified with Spirits

Coffee is an expression of hospitality throughout the world, and there is no better after-dinner relaxation than to enjoy the aromas of fragrant liqueurs and brandies blended with espresso.

The following is a list of several basic spirits with recipes and suggestions for creating your own personalized after-dinner entertainment ideas.

Unsweetened Spirits

Brandy / Cognac
Whiskeys:
 * Bourbon
 * Canadian
 * Irish
 * Scotch
Vodka

Coffee Liqueurs
Irish Creme
Kahlua
Tia Maria

Herb Flavored Liqueurs

Amaretto
Anisette
Benedictine
Drambuie
Galliano
Sambuca
Strega

Chocolate Flavor
Chocolate Mint
Creme de Cocoa

Orange Flavored Liqueurs

Cointreau
Curacao
Grand Marnier
Triple Sec

Fruit Flavors
Calvados

Flavored Spirits
Rock & Rye
Rum
Southern Comfort

Espresso With Spirits

Pre-heat cups and glasses with steam to retain heat. Add spirits to the cup or glass first, then prepare the espresso serving. Add other flavoring, sugar to taste, topping or garnish, and serve.

When entertaining you may wish to pre-heat your cups in a pan of hot water on the stove while preparing your espresso. For large groups, prepare several servings of espresso in advance. When using whipping cream, freshly whipped cream will last longer, since aerosol dispensed cream tends to melt as soon as it hits the hot espresso.

Remember that most iced espresso drinks are similar to the hot version and, therefore, most of the following drinks can also be served cold by fortifying the espresso serving and adding ice in a tall glass. By blending these same drinks with ice in a blender they become a frothy summertime cooler, similar to granitas.

All proportions are for one serving and subject to variation according to taste. A "dash" is roughly 10 drops, or a short spurt.

Caffè Puncino

Using an espresso cup, add 1-1/2 ounces of espresso to a dash of unsweetened spirits or rum. Add sugar to taste, and serve with a lemon peel, if desired.

Caffè Sambuca

Using an espresso cup, add 1-1/2 ounces of espresso to a dash of Sambuca. Always served with three (not two or four) coffee beans on a saucer for good luck. Originally a clear liqueur, black Sambuca is now served with white chocolate covered espresso beans as a gourmet touch to the classic Italian after-dinner drink.

Caffè Mexicana

Using a five-ounce cappuccino cup or glass, add one ounce espresso to one ounce each of Kahlua, cocoa, and heavy cream. Add sugar and vanilla to taste. Blend and heat with steam. Top with frothed milk and serve.

Irish Coffee

Prepare thickened cream by whipping fresh cream until it thickens but can still be poured. Using a large tall glass add two ounces espresso to 1-1/2 ounces Irish whiskey and sugar to taste. Gently pour the thickened cream over an inverted spoon to float the cream on the surface of the espresso. Sip the espresso through the cold layer of whipped cream.

Coffee Grog

Rub the inside of a cappuccino cup with butter, add 1-1/2 ounces espresso, to 1/2 ounce rum, 1/2 ounce brandy, add cloves and brown sugar to taste. Garnish with a cinnamon stick or nutmeg.

Caffè Calypso

In a five-ounce pre-heated cappuccino cup, add 3/4 ounces Tia Maria and 1/4 ounce Jamaican rum. Brew a two ounce serving of espresso into the cup, and top with frothed milk.

Café à l'Orange

In a small bowl, beat 1/2 cup whipping cream until stiff, fold in one tablespoon of powdered sugar, and chill. Prepare four espresso servings in pre-heated cappuccino cups and stir two tablespoons of Cointreau into each cup. Top with the chilled whipped cream and garnish with cinnamon.

Café Bourdaloue

Prepare a short (ristretto) espresso serving in a pre-heated espresso cup. Add 1/2 ounce anisette with 1/2 ounce crème de cacao.

Espresso Florentine

Pour one ounce of Amaretto in a pre-heated cappuccino cup. Brew a double (doppio) espresso serving into the cup. Top with whipped cream, garnish with nutmeg, and serve with an orange slice on the saucer.

Nikolai's con Panna

Pour 1/2 ounce vodka and one ounce Grand Marnier in a pre-heated cappuccino cup. Brew a double (doppio) espresso serving into the cup. Top with whipped cream and pour 1/2 teaspoon honey over the cream. Garnish with cinnamon.

Entertaining Ideas

Espresso with liqueur is an excellent digestive after a good meal, whether impressing a new client or relaxing with good friends. This selection of recipes suggests a special occasion or larger gathering due to the longer preparation.

Café Royale (serves six)

Prepare six servings of fresh espresso and six snifters of Cognac with six small sugar cubes and six tablespoons. Have your guests place a sugar cube on the spoon and fill it with cognac. Hold the spoon over the coffee to warm the Cognac and light with a match. When the flame subsides, stir the Cognac into the coffee. Brandy, Calvados or rum can be substituted for Cognac.

Espresso Brûlot (serves six)

An hour before serving, pour 1 ounce Galliano, 1 ounce Curacao and 1-1/2 ounces brandy into a deep saucepan. Add 6 lemon peel and 6 orange peel, 6 whole allspice, 4 whole cloves and 2 cinnamon sticks broken in half. Heat this mixture over a low heat. Slowly warming releases the flavors in the spices but a heat too high will evaporate the alcohol. Turn off the heat. Just before serving, heat the liqueurs again. Brew six servings of fresh espresso. When the liqueurs are hot, light with a match to flame for one or two minutes. Pour the espresso into the saucepan and reheat but do not boil. Spoon the espresso brûlot into demi-tasse cups adding 1 piece of lemon and orange peel to each serving.

Pousse-Café

This colorful French cordial is an impressive companion to after-dinner espresso and has recently made a comeback, although bartenders are not too fond of preparing pousse-café.

Assorted liqueurs are slowly poured over an inverted spoon to float the combination of different colors in layers, and pouring slowly over the inverted spoon keeps each layer separated. Pour heavier liqueurs first, such as Crème de cassis, Crème de banane, Crème de menthe, Crème de cacao, or blue Curacao. Lighter liqueurs, such as Triple Sec, Rock and Rye, B&B, Sloe gin and Kirsch, are poured last over the inverted spoon.

Accessories

Espresso should be served in a 2- to 2-1/2 ounce cup of thick porcelain or ceramicware to retain heat. Some demi-tasse cups are light-weight porcelain which does not retain heat as well as the traditional, heavier Italian-type demi-tasse.

Demi-tasse spoons are readily available in a variety of finishes, usually sold in sets of six or 12. The demi-spoon is a scaled down teaspoon to accompany a demi-tasse cup and saucer.

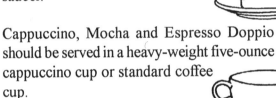

Cappuccino, Mocha and Espresso Doppio should be served in a heavy-weight five-ounce cappuccino cup or standard coffee cup.

Caffè Latte, Breve and Steamers are normally served in larger cups, from nine- to 12-ounce capacities.

Steaming or frothing pitchers are available in both stainless steel and ceramicware, in capacities from 1/3 liter (10 ounces) to one liter (33 ounces). The size recommended for home use is from 10 to 20 ounces. A refrigerated stainless steel frothing pitcher will help improve the froth for cappuccino.

Thermometers that clip onto the
frothing pitcher are available, and
they help gauge the status of
steaming or frothing below the
scalding point. Eventually you
will recognize the froth forming
(or dissipating if overheated) and
identify the high-pitched screech of
milk scalding. In the initial stages, a
thermometer may help while you refine your frothing and
steaming techniques.

Preparing espresso can be a somewhat messy process, so grounds
trays are a convenient accessory.
Also called a knock-box, the
grounds tray is divided into two
sections by a tamping bar used to
strike the filter holder and neatly
dispose of the grounds in one of the
two sections. The use of a grounds tray also insures the coffee
basket is not accidentally thrown away if dislodged from the filter
holder when tamping in a garbage bin.

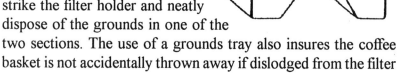

A flat bottom tamper is recommend to insure an even level bed of
espresso in the coffee basket. Some
manufacturers include a tamper with the
machine, and some machines feature a
built-in tamper. A hand-held tamper has
two sides to accommodate different filter
holders. However, tampers are not
universal. If not included with your
machine, make sure you purchase a flat-
bottom tamper that fits securely into the
filter holder.

The grinder brush can be a handy tool for burr grinder owners. The oils brought to the surface of the coffee bean in the roasting process cause ground coffee to accumulate around the grinding mechanism. The oily residue can eventually turn rancid and taint the delicate espresso flavor. Brushing the burrs with a stiff grinder brush will also remove traces of different blends of espresso roast.

CARE
AND
MAINTENANCE

CARE & MAINTENANCE OF YOUR ESPRESSO MACHINE

Your espresso machine should be kept immaculately clean in order to function properly and consistently produce flavorful espresso with crema, frothy cappuccino and smooth caffè latte. Coffee, especially a dark roast like espresso, imparts a gummy residue and oils that can eventually taint the espresso flavor. These residues and oils collect in the coffee grinder, the filter holder, coffee baskets, and especially in the brew head both under and over the shower disk (refer to Periodic Brew Head Cleaning).

Before cleaning your machines, be sure to unplug the unit from the electrical outlet and allow the machine to cool down completely. Remove and empty the water from the reservoir, rinse with water and let air dry (cloth or paper towels leave fibers that may be drawn into the pump). Remove the drip tray and drip pan, drain and wash thoroughly.

All removable parts that come in contact with the coffee, such as the filter holder and coffee baskets, should be washed in hot water, thoroughly rinsed and dried. If you use a mild detergent, be sure to rinse these components completely, since a residual film of soap can taint the espresso flavor. Do not use a harsh soap, detergent, or abrasive to clean these components. Using the dishwasher for any components of the espresso machine is not recommended due to the harsh detergents and high heat in the drying cycle.

Never immerse the body of the espresso machine or grinder in water. Wipe the machine housing with a soft, damp cloth, but do not use chemical cleaners, steel wool pads, or other abrasive materials.

It is strongly recommended that after each espresso brewing session you flush hot water through both the brew head and steam pipe. This is accomplished by priming or ventilating the system through both the brew head and steam pipe, as described in Chapter 6 on pages 87 and 88. Priming flushes out most of the coffee residue from the brew head and shower disk and evacuates any milk that may have been drawn into the steam pipe.

With a piston lever system, at the end of every session, after turning off the machine, open the steam valve to relieve any pressure remaining in the boiler. This will keep the internal gaskets from deforming.

The bottom surface of the shower disk should also be wiped with a damp cloth to remove any accumulation of coffee residue. If oils clog the perforated holes in the shower disk, this prevents the even saturation of the ground coffee in the filter holder and affects the quality of your espresso.

DECALCIFYING

One of the most common causes of espresso machine service problems is the accumulation of calcium and mineral deposits in the internal working components of an espresso machine. This problem is similar to calcification of a steam iron, especially in areas with hard water where mineral deposits can clog the plumbing system and block the flow of water or steam.

Remember that an espresso serving is roughly 98% water, and the quality of the water affects extraction of crema. If your water supply has a high mineral content, commonly referred to as hard water, we strongly recommend that you use filtered or bottled water to eliminate the build up of calcium or mineral deposits. (Use filtered or bottled water, but not distilled water since distilled water is flat and has no taste). The use of bottled water will always improve the flavor of your espresso, especially in areas where the water supply is highly chlorinated.

The use of bottled water for a thermal block system is even more important, since the small channels in the thermal block will quickly accumulate calcium deposits with the use of tap water. Aluminum alloy boilers are also prone to calcium build up, while brass and stainless steel boilers are not quite as sensitive.

Your espresso machine should be decalcified periodically, and the frequency depends on the mineral content of your water supply and how often you use your espresso machine. If you note the brewing and steaming power has diminished, this may indicate that calcium and mineral deposits are in the system.

There are several commercial espresso machine decalcifiers on the market designed for both drip coffee makers and espresso brewing systems. Please refer to your Owner's Manual before decalcifying your machine, since there will undoubtedly be some instructions provided by the manufacturer for your particular machine. Some manufacturers recommend two tablespoons of distilled white vinegar to each pint of water in the water reservoir.

Professionals caution against the overuse of vinegar or commercial decalcifiers that can damage the machine. They recommend the use of a very small amount of decalcifier on a regular basis, since vinegar or harsh chemicals can deteriorate gaskets inside the machine that will eventually cause leakage.

Once you have added the solution to your water reservoir, remove the filter holder and flush the solution through the both brew head and steam pipe, following the instructions for priming your system (Chapter 6 pages 87 and 88). It may be necessary to repeat this process several times to completely remove the mineral and calcium deposits that may have accumulated in the brewing system.

After decalcifying your system, rinse the water reservoir and refill with fresh, cold water. Use the same priming procedure through both the brew head and steam pipe to remove all traces of the decalcifying solution. Again, it may be necessary to repeat this process several times with fresh water.

PERIODIC BREW HEAD CLEANING

One of the most important maintenance procedures is the periodic cleaning of the brew head and perforated shower disk. The frequency depends on how often you use your espresso machine.

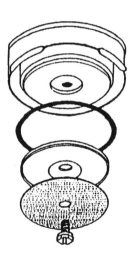

Espresso coffee produces a gummy residue that collects between the bottom of the brew head and the perforated shower disk.

This residue can clog the shower disk perforations and completely restrict the even saturation of the espresso grind. This residue may also taint the flavor and make it difficult to extract espresso with crema.

You can tell when some of the perforations are clogged by observing the flow of water through the shower disk while priming your system through the brew head without the filter holder in place. If water does not flow through the brew head evenly, the perforations of the shower disk may be clogged.

To clean the brew head and shower disk, most manufacturers recommend that you carefully remove the center screw or bolt with a screw driver or wrench. Do not force the screw, which can strip the threads. If the screw is difficult to turn, switch the Power On and allow the brew head to heat up. Be careful; the parts will be hot.

Clean the perforated shower disk under hot running water, or immerse it in boiling water in a saucepan. Re-assemble per the instructions provided in your instruction manual.

To retain a tight seal between the filter holder and brew head, do not store the filter holder in the brew head when the machine is not in use. Should the brew head gasket become deformed, allowing leakage around the filter holder in the brewing process, the gasket can be replaced following the same procedure for removing the shower disk.

It is important to always follow the manufacturer's instructions in your Owner's Manual when removing or reassembling the shower disk or brew head gasket of your machine.

HELPFUL HINTS

The use of filtered or bottled water is strongly recommended to improve the taste of your espresso and reduce calcification in your machine. Distilled water should not be used because it is flat and tasteless.

Ventilate fresh water liberally through the system each time the machine is used. In addition to pre-heating the system before use, priming after each use also flushes the system to reduce the accumulation of coffee residue in the brew head and any milk residue in the steam pipe.

Clean the bottom of the brew head with a wet cloth to remove accumulated coffee residue that transfers from the filter holder and coffee basket to the bottom of the shower disk in the brew head. Be careful if the brew head is hot.

If the flow of water through the brew head slows after a period of time, it may be necessary to remove and clean the perforated shower disk. Follow the manufacturer's instructions and refer to Periodic Brew Head Cleaning on page 142.

Wipe all traces of milk from the steam pipe after each use. Heat alters the proteins in milk, and, once it hardens, milk becomes difficult to remove. If the steam pipe is coated with milk, soak the steam pipe in a pitcher of water overnight, propped up to immerse the pipe in the water and soften the hardened milk. Or, "froth" water in a steaming pitcher to soften the milk coating.

Allow a short burst of steam to flow through the steam pipe to evacuate any milk that may have been drawn up into the steam vent when frothing or steaming milk. If the volume of steam diminishes after time, this may mean that milk has solidified in the steam vent pipe. If priming through the steam pipe does not remove the hardened milk, remove the steam nozzle and clean out the steam pipe with a thin wire.

Soak the filter holder and coffee baskets occasionally in a solution of one-part vinegar to five-parts water to remove all coffee residue, rinsing thoroughly with hot water.

To maintain a tight seal between the filter holder and brew head, do not store the filter holder in the brew head when the machine is not in use. This may deform the brew head gasket and, without a tight seal in the delivery group, coffee may spurt from around the filter holder in the brewing mode. Important: Please read the Owner's Manual included with your machine. Always follow the instructions and safeguards provided by the manufacturer /importer of your machine.

COLD WEATHER CAUTION

A pump-boiler espresso system should not be subjected to temperatures below freezing, unless most, if not all, water has been drained from the boiler. This is a little known fact, but one we discovered the hard way in shipping units to trade shows in sub-zero temperatures.

Because water expands when it freezes, the boiler itself or other boiler fittings could rupture as a result of this expansion. Occurrences of this particular problem would be leaving the espresso machine in the trunk of a car for prolonged periods in sub-zero weather, an unheated summer cottage during winter months, a relocation from one climate to another, or shipping a machine for service in a cold climate during the winter months.

There is no simple way to drain the boiler in a home espresso machine. Therefore, it becomes necessary to dissipate the water in the boiler through the steaming process. Follow the steps outlined for frothing, and evacuate all of the water from the machine boiler. It may take several minutes for the steam to completely dissipate. Be sure to turn Off the Power as soon as all the water is evaporated to protect the pump from overheating with an empty boiler. In the case of a pump-thermal block system, this procedure is not necessary because there is no retention of water in the thermal block.

HELP
SUPPORT
AND
RESOURCES

HELP, SUPPORT & RESOURCES

After-sales service of espresso equipment can be a headache. As an example, it is extremely frustrating to find that you inadvertently dumped your coffee basket in the trash bin and desperately need to order a replacement part. This is especially aggravating if you have misplaced or lost your owner's manual with the name, address and phone number of the importer or manufacturer of your machine.

A more serious situation, of course, is if the pump burns out or the machine malfunctions. It then becomes a question of locating a service center authorized by the manufacturer to repair your espresso machine.

Most espresso equipment for home use is manufactured abroad. The manufacturer has either established their own U.S.-based organization to handle the distribution and after-sales service of their equipment, or they have appointed a U.S. importer. An alphabetical list follows with the most recognized home espresso machine brand names and the associated manufacturer or importer with their U.S. address and telephone number.

Do not attempt to repair your machine. If you cannot resolve the problem after reviewing your owner's manual, you should call the manufacturer/importer customer service department and explain the problem.

If the problem cannot be resolved over the phone, they will refer you to a factory authorized service center.

All home espresso machines sold in North America carry what is called a limited warranty, usually in effect for one year from the date of purchase. The word limited indicates that the warranty covers only defects in material or workmanship, and the manufacturer or importer has the option to repair or replace the unit without charge within a specific period of time.

A limited warranty would be void by what is called customer abuse, caused by damage to the product by accident or misuse by the consumer. One of the most common causes of customer abuse is allowing the water reservoir to run dry, which can burn out the pump.

Dropping the machine and cracking the housing, breaking the water reservoir, or losing the filter holder are not covered under the limited warranty. The limited warranty may be void if a machine intended for home use is used in a semi-commercial environment, such as a small café or delicatessen.

Many manufacturers and importers of home espresso machines provide specific instructions in their owner's manual to resolve common malfunctions of a machine. In some cases they will be able to troubleshoot over the phone. If not, they may require that the machine be carefully packed and shipped to their factory authorized service center.

If you are not certain of the procedure for repair of your particular machine, we recommend that you call the manufacturer/importer for more specific instructions. The following tips will help expedite the repair and return of your machine:

* Keep all removable parts at home to avoid further damage in transit. Pack the appliance carefully, in the original carton, if possible.

* Tape a legible note to the body of the machine with your name, address, phone number, and a brief explanation of the problem.

* To insure in-warranty service. you may need to provide the date or proof of purchase. Repair work on equipment out-of-warranty is usually billed for materials, labor, and return shipping charges.

It should be noted that European manufacturers occasionally change their U.S. importers. A machine you purchased six years ago may now be handled by a different importer. The list of manufacturers and/or importers is, to our knowledge, the most current as of the publication of this book.

Independent Service Centers

As you can see from the "anatomy" diagrams, espresso equipment is relatively sophisticated with a number of small parts, and even more are shown in detail on an engineering explosion drawing. Repairing espresso equipment is unlike the repair of a drip coffee maker, iron, vacuum cleaner, or sewing machine. In addition, even filter holders and coffee baskets are not interchangeable between different brands of equipment. It would be impossible for any one service center to maintain a complete parts inventory on all brands of espresso equipment.

If you cannot locate the manufacturer or importer of your machine for factory authorized service, two very reputable independent service centers are: Freed, Teller & Freed in San Francisco, phone (415) 673-0922; and Home Espresso Repair in Seattle, phone (206) 789-9513. Both maintain parts and specialize in certain equipment, but they will refer you to another source if they cannot order parts or repair your machine.

ESPRESSO MACHINE MANUFACTURERS & IMPORTERS

BRAND	COMPANY	CITY/STATE	PHONE
Bosch	Robert Bosch Corp.	Broadview, IL	(708) 865-5265
Braun	Braun, Inc.	Lynnfield, MA	(617) 596-7300
Briel	Briel America, Inc.	Livingston, NJ	(800) 763-6699
Capresso	Capresso, Inc.	Harrington Park, NJ	(201) 767-3999
DeLonghi	DeLonghi America, Inc.	Carlstadt, NJ	(201) 507-1110
Faema	Faema Corp. of America	Fairfield, CT	(203) 334-7100
Gaggia	Lello Appliances, Inc.	E. Rutherford, NJ	(201) 939-2555
Krups	Krups North America	Closter, NJ	(201) 767-5500
LaPavoni	European Gift & Hswrs	Bronx, NY	(718) 325-5397
Maxim	Maxim Company	Mt. Prospect, IL	(708) 803-4600
Melitta	Melitta USA, Inc.	Cherry Hill, NJ	(609) 428-7202
Mr. Coffee	Mr. Coffee, Inc.	Bedford Hts., OH	(216) 464-4000
Piccola	Xcell Corporation	Westont, IL	(800) 722-7751
Rancilio	Saeco U.S.A., Inc.	Saddle Brook, NJ	(800) 437-6874
Rotel	Saeco U.S.A., Inc.	Saddle Brook, NJ	(800) 437-6874
Rowenta	Rowenta, Inc.	Cambridge, MA	(617) 661-1600
Saeco	Saeco U.S.A., Inc.	Saddle Brook, NJ	(800) 437-6874
Salton	Salton Houswares Group	Mt. Prospect, IL	(708) 803-4600
Solis	Solis America, Inc.	Allendale, NJ	(201) 236-1818

THE
ESPRESSO
ENCYCLOPEDIA

aerator Device attached to the steam vent pipe that aerates milk by inducing additional air into the flow of steam. Using the same principal as a kitchen faucet aerator, more air in the jet of steam creates more bubbles in the milk to increase the volume rapidly and "froth" the milk.

Some aerators form large bubbles in the milk that tend to dissipate quickly, while other aerators create a denser froth with smaller bubbles or foam.

Aerators are also available with a siphon hose that draws milk directly from the milk container and dispenses frothed milk into a cappuccino cup.
Important: keep the aerator clean since, heating milk alters the proteins and hardened milk is difficult to remove.

acidity Related to coffee, acidity is an attribute, not a sour or bitter taste. Coffee with acidity usually indicates a pleasantly sharp and "snappy" quality, characteristic of high-grown arabica beans.

atmosphere (ATM)   Unit of measuring pump pressure; one atm (atmosphere) equals 14.69 psi (pounds per square inch) of pump pressure. The preferred pump pressure for a home espresso machine is between 9 and 17 ATMS (x 14.69 = 132 to 250 psi).

The pressure will vary depending on the fineness of the grind, which provides the resistance to the water to extract espresso. The European term for ATM is Bar for barometric pressure.

arabica (coffea arabica)   A coffee bean that originated in Ethiopia, noted for its intense, aromatic flavor. Used in specialty coffees, arabica beans are lower in caffeine, more expensive, and have more flavor and aroma than "robusta" beans. Arabica beans are also called high-grown because the coffee trees are grown 2,000 feet above sea level.

Americano An espresso that resembles drip coffee by adding hot water from the steam pipe to dilute the serving but preserve the espresso flavor. This should not mean overextracting espresso by allowing more water to flow through the brew head. In Italy "Americano" refers to an espresso lungo or long pull. Europeans often refer to "Americano" as the espresso served in many American restaurants, meaning an overextracted serving compared to European standards.

bar   The unit of measure used in Europe for pump pressure as opposed to atmospheres (ATM) or psi. Barometric pressure is slightly less than atmospheric pressure, and one bar is very close to one ATM of pressure.

Barista Italian word for one who has mastered the espresso machine, and an expert on brewing and mixing espresso beverages.

back pressure release valve A solenoid valve triggered when the brewing cycle has stopped to relieve pressure away from the brew head and filter holder. The solenoid opens a valve that redirects the pressurized water in the brew head and releases it into the drip tray. This feature is commonly incorporated in commercial equipment, and a few of the more expensive home espresso machines now feature a back pressure release valve.

bistro Originally a small French café without seating, where counter-height tables are arranged for a fast beverage. A bistro(t) is usually found in commercial areas with heavy traffic or airports and train stations. Said to have originated from Russian soldiers in Paris abruptly ordering coffee "bistro, bistro" (hurry) who would drink up and run.

blend Mixing two or more straight coffees (varietals) from different origins after the beans have been roasted. Different roasts (lighter and darker) are blended either by the roaster or specialty coffee retailer, and, with a quality roast, the blend is a matter of personal taste. "House Blend" refers to the special blend a roaster or retailer has developed by mixing different beans to their preference.

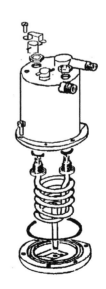

boiler A closed vessel used to heat water or generate steam in espresso machines. Home espresso machines are available in a variety of boiler sizes, and the capacity is measured in milliliters. Boilers are constructed of aluminum, stainless steel, brass, or copper. The capacity and material used to construct the boiler impact on the cost and operation of the espresso machine.

brew head   The brewing chamber that holds the filter holder in place and dispenses water through the espresso grind. The brew head with the filter holder is called the delivery group. A fine espresso grind tamped in the coffee basket is placed in the filter holder, and the filter holder is inserted into the brew head. The delivery group builds up pressure and dispenses water through the espresso grind. The brew head is attached to the bottom of the boiler or thermal block with the shower disk and gaskets to create a tight seal around the filter holder when brewing espresso. See Delivery Group and Group.

burr(s)   Two corrugated steel cylindrical plates with cutting edges used in coffee grinders to slice or shave the coffee bean to a consistent grind. The top burr is stationary and the bottom burr rotates. An electric burr grinder uses a motor to control the speed of the burrs, reducing heat and dissipation of coffee oils in grinding.

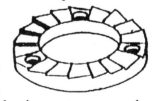

Burr grinders are adjustable from a coarse grind (burrs further apart) to a very fine grind (burrs closer together). The burrs control the consistency of the grind by maintaining the index or distance between the burrs. Deeper cone burrs and a gear reduction motor are used in commercial grinders to increase the variance of the grind and reduce heat in the grinding process.

brûlot   An elegant mixture of liqueurs heated and flamed, served with espresso to entertain after dinner. See "Espresso Brûlot" under Recipes.

C

Caffè Latte   Italian term for a double serving of espresso with steamed milk. Café au Lait in French, Café con Leche in Spanish, and Kaffee mit Milch in

12 OUNCE LATTE CUP

German, the caffè latte serving is roughly one-third espresso to two-thirds steamed milk, served in a large nine-ounce bowl-shaped cup or wide-mouthed glass. Lattes are also embellished with flavorings added before the espresso, or steamed with milk.

caffeine   An alkaloid found in the leaves and berries of coffee, chemically identical with theine (an alkaloid found in the tea plant); used as a stimulant and diuretic. Espresso coffee has less caffeine because arabica beans are used (less than half the caffeine of robusta beans) and usually roasted longer (darker), which further reduces the caffeine content.

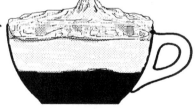

cappuccino   Usually equal thirds of espresso, steamed milk, and frothed milk served in a five-ounce cappuccino cup. Steamed milk at the bottom of the frothing pitcher is poured over the espresso, and the

5 OUNCE CAPPUCCINO CUP

froth at the top of the pitcher is spooned on top to "cap" the cappuccino and retain the heat. Cappuccino is often garnished with a light sprinkle of chocolate or cocoa, cinnamon, nutmeg, vanilla powder or colored sugar crystals.

Capuchin   An Italian religious order of monks distinguished by their brown hooded robes, said to have discovered cappuccino as a recipe using "coffea arabica" with milk in a drink that helped keep them awake during prayer sessions. The color of their drink matched the color of their robes.

coffee basket(s) Also called filter baskets, or brew baskets, the coffee baskets are usually stainless steel in one- and two-cup sizes. The bottom of the coffee basket has small perforations that filter water through the espresso grind, restricting the ground coffee from passing through the coffee basket. Some espresso machines provide a universal coffee basket built into the filter holder to brew both single and double servings. Care should be taken to insure the coffee basket perforations are not clogged with coffee residue, which can restrict the flow of water through the filter holder.

colloid A gelatin-like liquid measure with very fine suspended particles that result in a very slow rate of sedimentation. The oils in a fine espresso grind form colloids that develop the golden crema encrusting the top of a properly brewed espresso serving. Overextracting espresso releases bitter oils that break down the colloids and dissipate the crema.

combination machine An espresso machine with a built-in automatic drip coffee maker. The espresso portion can be a non-pump or pump-driven system, and the drip coffee system operates independently or simultaneously with the espresso/cappuccino functions.

crema Often referred to as foam ("schiuma" in Italian), crema is unique to espresso. It is visual evidence that espresso has been brewed properly. Crema is the foamy, golden brown extraction that develops in the filter holder and encrusts the top of an espresso serving. It is visible, smooth and creamy, with a fresh, bittersweet taste not found in other types of coffee. The Italians claim a true crema should hold the granules of a teaspoon of sugar on top of the espresso serving before the sugar slowly descends to the bottom of the cup.

decaf decaffeination Technically, at least 97% of the caffeine must be removed from the coffee bean for the label to indicate "decaffeinated". Decaffeinated beans are more difficult to roast, and the cost is slightly higher due to the extra handling involved in the decaffeination process. It is a challenge to remove the caffeine from the beans and not remove the coffee flavor. Caffeine is water soluble and, by soaking the green coffee beans in water, solvents are used to separate the caffeine from the water. The water with the coffee flavor is added back to the beans with at least 97% of the caffeine removed.

decalcification decalcify Decalcifying an espresso machine eliminates calcium deposits that collect inside the boiler and/or thermal block, which will eventually clog the brewing and steaming process. A decalcifier solution is used to break down calcium deposits and flush them from the espresso system. Areas with very hard water will require more frequent decalcification, based on how often the machine is in use. Bottled (not distilled) or filtered water is recommended to avoid the build-up of calcium deposits.

delivery group   The combination of the brew head, gasket assembly, shower disk, and filter holder together that contain the pressure and extract espresso from the ground coffee, delivering espresso into the cup. See Group

demi-tasse   French term for "half cup" used to serve a 1-1/2 ounce single espresso in a 2-1/2 cup. In Europe, dinnerware has always been sold with a choice of two cup sizes, five-ounce tasse (our "coffee" cup) and demi-tasse. Dinnerware sold here now offers both size cups, another example of the growing popularity of espresso in North America.

doppio   (Espresso Doppio) Double serving of espresso, usually three to four ounces, using the two-cup coffee basket in the filter holder for one double serving of espresso in a five-ounce cup.

doser   Mechanism attached to burr grinders that dispenses a pre-measured "dose" of espresso grind directly into the filter holder. One sweep of the lever pushes a pre-measured single serving (usually 7 grams) into the filter holder, and two sweeps of the lever push a double serving of ground espresso.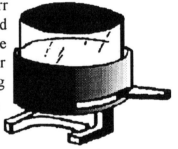
The amount of coffee can be adjusted to your personal taste.

dwell time   The recovery time required for the thermostats to establish the functional temperature. Dwell time refers to the period of time it takes to raise the temperature from brewing up to steam, or from the steam temperature back below boiling for brewing.

Pump-driven espresso machines have at least two thermostats: one that controls the temperature under boiling for brewing espresso and a second that maintains the temperature well above boiling for generating steam.

The dwell time in home espresso equipment can vary by machine from 30 seconds to three minutes. This differentiates home espresso machines from commercial equipment, since commercial machines have no dwell time and maintain the two separate temperatures simultaneously.

espresso   A method of quickly extracting the heart of the coffee flavor under pressure in single servings, usually 1-1/2 ounce. Some believe the origin of the word is from the French "exprès," especially for you, while others believe the Italian "espresso," for fast, is the source. Regardless of its origin, the result is a beverage served in individual portions with premium flavor known around the world as espresso. The many elements required to extract a true espresso with crema are well worth the effort.

extraction   The brewing cycle in preparing espresso that can be timed (drawn for 20 seconds) or judged by the color of the coffee (developing a golden brown foam or crema) while brewing into the espresso cup(s). The extraction is critical. Overextracting allows too much water to pass through the grind, extracting bitter oils that break down the colloids and dissipate the crema.

fazenda   Portuguese term for farm. Coffee fazenda in Brazil means a coffee plantation.

filter holder   The portable handle that holds a filter and fits into the brew head, where water is dispensed through the ground coffee in the filter holder. Also called the "porta-filter", the filter holder brewing basket accepts the coffee (filter) basket that holds the ground coffee.

Several manufacturers have developed special filter holder or coffee basket systems that further restrict the flow of water through the espresso grind, ensuring an even saturation of the coffee and building additional pressure within the delivery group.

The filter holder has two spouts or spigots that should be centered over one cup for a single serving or centered over two cups side-by-side for brewing two individual servings of espresso from a two-cup filter (coffee) basket. Commercial machines are often equipped with two separate porta-filters, one with a single spout and a "double" with two spouts that holds twice as much coffee.

flip drip pot   Also called the Neopolitan or macchinetta (little machine), the stove-top flip drip pot uses the same gravity brewing principle as any drip coffee maker. Water is heated in one chamber, then inverted or flipped over the coffee chamber and seeped through the coffee into the serving chamber. A Neopolitan has a unique double handle design, one for the coffee chamber and the other for the serving chamber. Originally from Naples, the Neopolitan is available in sizes from two- to 12-cup capacities and produces a strong drip coffee on the stove top.

French roast   Not the origin of the beans, French roast is a degree of dark roast. On the West Coast of the United States, some consider a French roast to be the darkest, while on the East Coast some consider an Italian roast to be the darkest roast.

French roasted beans can range from light dark brown with a shiny surface to almost black with an oily surface, depending how the beans were roasted.

froth   Aerated milk with a foamy texture that has been aerated or "frothed" in a frothing pitcher for cappuccino. Steam from the steam pipe aerates the milk and creates small, tight bubbles that form the froth. Scalding or overheating milk will ruin the froth, much like a fallen soufflé.

The froth forms a "cap" on top of a cappuccino serving to retain the heat of the espresso and steamed milk beneath the froth.

full city roast   Term for a roast of coffee that originated in New York meaning a medium dark roast (city roast) where the beans are roasted to full development (full city roast). The beans are medium brown in color with a dry surface and mild, smooth taste.

granita   Italian term for a refreshing frozen flavored syrup dessert, similar to an espresso sorbet. Commercial granita machines keep ice and flavored syrups rotating to prevent the ingredients from solidifying.

Granita lattes are served as an iced drink in a wide variety of flavors and can also be prepared at home starting with espresso ice cubes in a blender.

grinder   The machine that grinds coffee beans in a variety of ways. Handheld mills, blade grinders and burr grinders are available for home use. Espresso requires a consistent, fine grind, and a burr grinder is recommended.

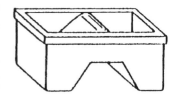

A hand grinder manually rotates two burrs and, with some effort, will grind consistently fine for espresso. Blade grinders work well for coarser grinds, for drip coffee, stove-top and electric non-pump machines, but the whirling blades offer no control over the consistency of the grind. With pump-driven espresso equipment, however, the consistency and fineness of the grind are critical in extracting espresso with crema.

grounds tray   A two-bin receptacle with a center bar for striking the filter holder and releasing the spent espresso pellet from the coffee basket. Also called a "knock" or "dump" box, the grounds tray can be convenient for clean-up, since espresso tends to be a very messy business. Also, if the coffee basket falls out of the filter holder when knocking out the used grounds, the coffee basket will land in the grounds tray and not the garbage, when the discovery is often too late.

group   The combination of the brew head, gasket assembly, shower disk, and filter holder together that contain the pump pressure and extract espresso from the ground coffee, delivering espresso into the cup.

Home espresso machines are single group. Commercial espresso machines are differentiated by the number of "groups"; a two-group or three-group machine. A three-group commercial machine can brew six servings of espresso at one time, two servings beneath each of the three delivery groups.

hacienda   Spanish term for farm or ranch, used in Venezuela for coffee plantation.

hand burr grinder   A manual version of an electric burr grinder where two burrs are rotated manually to grind coffee beans, and the ground coffee is collected in a drawer beneath the burrs. A handle controls the rotation of the burrs and has an adjustment nut to set the distance between the burrs and adjust from a very coarse to a very fine grind.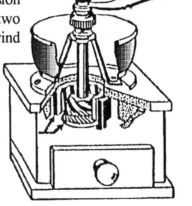

hazelnut   A hard-shelled nut from the hazel tree (birch family), also called a filbert, very popular in North America as a coffee flavoring in powder or liquid form.

heating element   An electrical device used to heat water in an espresso machine, usually controlled by thermostats to maintain one temperature for brewing and a higher temperature for generating steam.

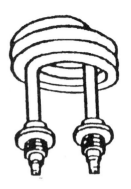

The heating element in a boiler system (non-pump, pump and piston lever) is located inside the boiler. In a pump-thermal block system, the heating element is molded into the thermal block, similar to the calrod heating element of an electric stove.

The thermal block flash-heats the water that the pump pulses through the channels machined into the thermal block for brewing and steaming. The length of the channels vary from 30" to 50", depending on the size of the thermal block.

heat exchanger   Commonly used in commercial espresso equipment and in some semi-commercial machines, where the boiler capacity is larger than home-use machines. The heat exchanger eliminates the dwell time between brewing and steam by simultaneously stabilizing the two temperatures using a separate water supply for brewing espresso from superheated water for generating steam.

A pipe or tube draws water directly into the heat exchanger located inside the boiler, feeding the brew head from a separate supply of fresh water in the brew mode at a thermostatically maintained temperature below boiling. Superheated water surrounding the heat exchanger in the boiler is maintained at a higher temperature for generating

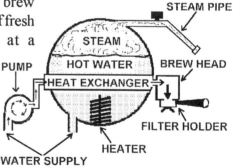

steam on demand. Large commercial machines have a heat exchanger for each delivery group.

hopper   The container located on top of most burr grinders that holds whole beans, usually tapered to feed the beans into the grinding mechanism. Whole beans should not be stored in the bean hopper.

hull (husk)   The parchment and silver skin surrounding each of two seeds inside the red coffee cherry. The two seeds inside the hull are the coffee beans. Hulling machines remove the parchment and silver skin to reveal two coffee beans from each red berry.

SKIN
PULP
PARCHMENT
SILVER SKIN
COFFEE BEAN

I

Italian roast   A degree of roast, not the origin of the coffee bean. Some consider an Italian roast to be darker than a French roast, and others consider a French roast the darkest. An Italian roast is usually a darker color (dark brown to almost black) with a shiny to oily surface indicating a longer roast, depending on the roaster. Italian roast is often associated with espresso, but the blend and roast are a matter of personal taste.

J

Java   An Indonesian island southeast of Sumatra where a type of coffee is grown. Java is now also recognized slang for coffee.

Kaldi The goat herder said to have discovered the benefits of coffee when he saw how lively his goats became after eating the berries from a special tree.

kiosk Originating as a Turkish word (kiushk) for an ornamental summerhouse. Kiosk has been adapted and modified to differentiate a retail stand selling one type of product (news stand) from a retail store that houses a collection of products. Commercial coffee carts in the malls of shopping centers are often referred to as kiosks.

Kona A district on the southwest side of the island of Hawaii that grows the best of Hawaiian coffee.

latte Italian word for milk and caffè latte for coffee with milk. Lattes served in North America are usually one-third espresso to two-thirds steamed milk, sometimes topped with a layer of froth, and also served here with flavored syrups. If you order just a "latte" in Italy, you will be served a glass of milk.

latteccino A recent innovation for a milk-based espresso beverage combining the consistency of a caffè latte (steamed milk) and cappuccino (steamed with equal part frothed milk). A latteccino can be considered a frothier latte or milkier cappuccino.

lungo   A "long pull" in Italian, allowing more water to flow through the ground espresso but still not overextracting the brew. An espresso lungo is roughly a two-ounce serving and should still have crema on top.

macchiato   Espresso Macchiato is a single serving of espresso "marked" with one or two tablespoons of frothed milk. A Latte Macchiato is a single serving of espresso poured into a glass of steamed milk to "mark" the milk with espresso.

macchinetta   See Flip Drip Pot and Neapolitan - Italian word for "little machine," used to prepare a strong drip coffee on the stove top.

Mexicana   Usually Kahlua flavor added to drip coffee or milk-based espresso drinks with heavy cream.

milk   Frothed and/or steamed milk are used in preparing espresso-based drinks such as cappuccino and caffè latte. Cold, fresh milk is important to improve the frothing process, and the fat content of the milk can also affect the froth.

Non-fat or 2% milk is easier to froth, but whole milk will develop a froth with more body. Half-and-half and cream will steam but will not develop a real froth because of the high butter fat content. Non-dairy alternatives, such as soy milk, are available for those allergic to milk.

mocha   A chocolate-flavored milk-based espresso drink with roughly 1/3 espresso brewed into 1/3 frothed milk where 1/3 cocoa has been dissolved. Other variations with chocolate include adding egg white or vanilla, mocha latte with all steamed milk, a dry mocha with only frothed milk, and flavored syrups added to the mocha for a variety of signature drinks.

Moka   Stove-top espresso maker with a distinctive shape, the Moka Express was invented in 1933 by Alfonso Bialetti in Italy. The Moka develops slight pressure from boiling water in a sealed chamber that rises through a tube, through a coffee basket, and into an upper chamber for serving.

Mokas are usually available in three, six, nine and 12-cup capacities made of aluminum or stainless steel.

Neapolitan   See Flip Drip Pot. A stove-top brewer originating from Naples where water is heated in one chamber and inverted or flipped over a coffee chamber. Water seeps through the coffee into a serving chamber that is disconnected from the coffee chamber for serving.

nozzle   The piece fitted to the end of the steam pipe where steam or hot water are released through the steam pipe. The nozzle has small holes or a slit that pressurizes the steam for frothing milk and steaming milk for cappuccino and lattes. The steam nozzle should be aerated and kept clean, since hardened milk can collect inside the nozzle and reduce the flow of steam through the steam pipe.

nutmeg   The aromatic kernel of the fruit from tropical trees with a distinctive flavor. Nutmeg is sold whole or ground, and ground nutmeg is used as a topping for cappuccino and lattes.

oils   The essence of espresso flavor is in the delicate oils of the coffee bean. The roasting process forces moisture out of the bean and brings volatile oils closer to the surface of the bean. The darker the roast, the longer the bean was roasted, and a dark roast has a shinier (oily) surface.

Darker roasts with an oilier surface dissipate flavor faster because the oils are closest to the bean surface. Very oily beans tend to stick together in the grinder and may gum up the grinder burrs and bean hopper, especially if very oily beans are refrigerated.

organic coffee   Organic beans are certified by U.S. government or independent agencies to be cultivated in areas free of pesticides and chemicals in the soil used to improve a coffee yield. Professionals debate the organic issue, from questioning the certification process to claiming organic beans lack flavor. Organic coffees are more expensive and growing in popularity.

overextraction   Allowing too much water to flow through a one- or two-cup coffee basket, overextracting the espresso and releasing some of the bitter oils. Overextracting ruins the flavor and dissipates the crema. In a restaurant, overextracted espresso with no crema should be refused. Either the restaurant feels their customer will feel cheated with less than a full cup of coffee, or the bartender was too busy to brew the espresso properly. Once you know what to look for in a crema espresso, you should not accept or pay for an overextracted espresso.

peaberry   A single round bean, instead of two flat beans, per coffee cherry. Most red coffee berries contain two seeds with flat sides facing each other. These are the coffee beans. But occasionally nature provides a single round bean, called a peaberry.

Piston Lever The forerunner to electric pump espresso machines, the piston lever is a boiler system still available on both the commercial and home espresso machine markets. The lever forces a piston down through a chamber and provides the necessary pressure (leverage) to force hot water through a fine espresso grind.

Piston lever machines are impressive and classic in design and will produce a crema espresso, frothy cappuccino and smooth caffè latte. The results from a piston lever machine tend to be more reliant on the operator and speed of manipulating the lever than more modern push-button machines.

Thermostats control the brewing and steaming temperatures. In the steam mode, a piston lever machine generates steam from the boiler vented through the top of the machine.

pods Pre-ground espresso in a mesh pellet that fit into the coffee basket of the filter holder for single servings (or stack two for double servings). Also available in decaf and, if sealed individually for freshness, pods are very convenient for spontaneous entertaining.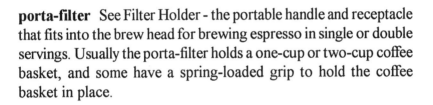

porta-filter See Filter Holder - the portable handle and receptacle that fits into the brew head for brewing espresso in single or double servings. Usually the porta-filter holds a one-cup or two-cup coffee basket, and some have a spring-loaded grip to hold the coffee basket in place.

Other porta-filters are made with one coffee basket for single or double espresso servings. Commercial espresso machines are often sold with two porta-filters; one with a single spout for single servings and a second with two spouts and larger filter basket for brewing two espresso servings.

pre-infusion Also referred to as "pre-soaking", some machines will automatically infuse a quantity of water into the filter holder before the pump forces the water through the fine espresso grind. Pre-infusion ensures the complete saturation of the coffee in the coffee basket for full flavor extraction. Pre-infusion is a common feature on commercial equipment, also available on some more expensive home espresso machines.

priming Also called ventilating, priming flushes fresh water through the espresso system to prime the pump, pre-heat the brew head and filter holder, and eliminate any air pockets that may be in the system.

Priming the system is key to proper maintenance of an espresso machine. Priming through the brew head flushes the shower disk of coffee residue, and priming through the steam pipe evacuates any milk that may be drawn up into the pipe when steaming.

psi Pounds-per-square-inch used to measure pump pressure, used in conjunction with atmospheres (ATM) where one ATM equals 14.69 pounds-per-square-inch of pump pressure. The water pressure supplied by most city water systems for the average kitchen faucet is 35 psi. The reciprocal pump in home machines produces pulsing pressure from 9 to 17 ATMS or 135 to 250 psi. See Atmosphere and Bar.

pump Home espresso machines use a reciprocal (pulsing) or in-line solenoid pump. Depending on its size, the pump delivers between 9 and 17 ATMS (or from 135 to 250 psi) of pump pressure.

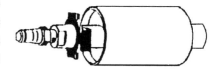

Pumps are also rated by wattage, and the average home espresso machine pump is from 50 to 70 watts. The pump is vital to provide the necessary pressure to quickly force the water through a fine grind and extract the true espresso flavor with crema.

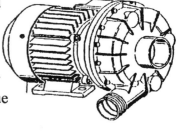

Commercial equipment uses a centrifugal pump, which is a larger pump with higher capacities for moving larger volume of water under constant pressure. A centrifugal pump in a commercial espresso machine delivers a constant 9 ATMS of pump pressure.

puncino An after-dinner single serving of espresso (1-1/2 ounces) where a dash or 10 drops of unsweetened spirits (brandy, cognac, whiskey, vodka) are added.

pyrolysis A critical point in the roasting process when the beans are removed from the roaster. Pyrolysis indicates a chemical change inside the beans when the surface darkens and oils develop that determine the degree of roast. The roasting process forces moisture from the bean, and the heat makes the bean expand and lose its weight. Coffee beans are roasted at over 400°F, and the roastmaster determines at what critical point the desired degree of roast is attained.

ready light Also called status lights, as the name implies the ready light signals when the water in the boiler or thermal block has reached the correct temperature for brewing espresso (in the coffee mode) or generating steam (in the steam mode). Some ready lights signal "ready" when the light goes on (usually a green light), and some machines signal "ready" when the light goes out (usually a red light).

The ready light may cycle on and off in the coffee or steam mode, which indicates the thermostat is maintaining the correct temperature for brewing espresso or generating steam. Not all machines have a ready light, which means the heating period for separate temperatures must be estimated. If the steaming temperature has not been reached, the first burst of steam will be weak and watery. If the correct brewing temperature has not been reached after generating steam, the espresso grind may be scalded by water at a temperature above 200°F.

ristretto A short or "restricted" espresso where the flow of water through the brew head is stopped at about 1 ounce. Ristretto macchiato is a short espresso "marked" with a teaspoon of frothed milk.

roast The process that forces moisture out of the green coffee bean and brings volatile oils closer to the surface of the bean. The darker the roast, the longer the bean was roasted, and a dark roast can have less caffeine than a lighter roast.

An espresso roast suggests the darkest bean and a bolder taste, but there is no official espresso blend or degree of roast. There are three basic types of roasts: Full City Roast, a light dark roast with a dry surface; Medium Dark Roast, darker brown in color with a slightly oily surface; and Dark Roast, the darkest color, shiniest surface and bolder taste.

The roasting process forces moisture out of the bean, and the heat makes it expand and lose weight. One pound of dark roasted beans will yield more volume than one pound of a lighter roast.

robusta A coffee bean species from the Congo region of Africa, called Coffea Canaphora. Robusta are beans grown at a lower elevation than arabica beans, cultivated for the heartiness of the tree. Robustas lack many of the desirable characteristics of high-grown arabica beans. Robusta is lower in price and mostly used by high volume coffee companies that blend robustas with a lesser amount of more flavorful and expensive arabica beans. Some roasters use robusta in their espresso blend due to its higher fat content that creates more crema. The caffeine content of robusta beans is double that of arabica, and there is no comparison in flavor.

romano A single serving of espresso served with a fresh lemon peel. Originally the lemon peel was used to rub around the rim and sanitize the cup, and some say the lemon peel was used to clean one's teeth after drinking the espresso. This is not an Italian custom, but espresso romano is often served in restaurants in North America. The lemon peel should be served on a saucer, not in the espresso, since the citrus acid will break down the colloids and dissipate any crema.

S

shower disk   A perforated disk at the bottom of the brew head that channels the pressurized water to "shower" the compressed grind and totally saturate the ground espresso. It is important that the shower disk be kept clean, since the perforations can become clogged with a gummy residue that will restrict the even saturation of the espresso. Refer to "Periodic Brew Head Cleaning" for instructions on cleaning the shower disk.

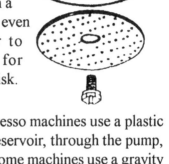

siphon hose Most pump-driven espresso machines use a plastic siphon hose to draw water from the reservoir, through the pump, and into the boiler or thermal block. Some machines use a gravity feed water reservoir and do not have a siphon hose, or the siphon hose is built into the machine.

It is important to make sure the siphon hose is immersed in the water supply and to not let the water reservoir run dry, or the siphon hose will draw air into the pump, which can cause damage.

spirits   Sweetened, unsweetened, herb, fruit and chocolate flavored liqueurs added to espresso for entertaining. Coffee is an expression of hospitality throughout the world, and there is no better after-dinner relaxation than the aroma of fragrant liqueurs and brandies (spirits) blended with espresso.

status lights   See ready lights - indicate the status of the thermostats in either the coffee brewing mode or steam mode.

steam pipe Also called the steam vent or steam wand, the steam pipe provides the outlet for steam generated in the boiler or thermal block to flow into the frothing pitcher.

The steam pipe also dispenses hot water when the machine is in the coffee mode (Coffee Switch On) with the Steam Valve open. It is important to aerate the steam vent after frothing or steaming to evacuate milk that may have been drawn into the steam pipe.

Also, wipe the steam pipe with a wet cloth after frothing or steaming milk, since hardened milk is difficult to remove. It may be necessary to "froth" water to soften any hardened milk residue on the steam pipe.

steam valve Controls the flow of steam through the steam pipe (vent or wand). In general, pump-boiler systems have adjustable steam control by turning the valve for more or less steam pressure.

Steam is generated at the top of the boiler, and opening the Steam Valve releases the encapsulated steam through the steam pipe. In a pump-boiler system, the pump does not operate in the steam mode.

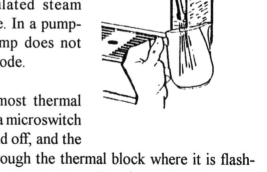

The Steam Valve in most thermal block systems triggers a microswitch to turn the steam on and off, and the pump pulses water through the thermal block where it is flash-heated above boiling to generate steam. In a thermal block system, the pump operates in the steam mode.

steamers   Cappuccino steamers or frothers do not brew coffee and only generate steam. Steamers range from stove-top models to semi-commercial pump-driven steamers. Water is heated above boiling to generate steam, and the steam is released by opening the adjustable Steam Valve. Steamers can also be used to heat 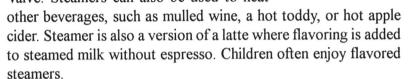 other beverages, such as mulled wine, a hot toddy, or hot apple cider. Steamer is also a version of a latte where flavoring is added to steamed milk without espresso. Children often enjoy flavored steamers.

stove-tops   Non-electric espresso makers that use a gas or electric stove as the heat source for brewing coffee. The Neapolitan and Moka machines are stove-top espresso makers that produce a strong drip coffee.

tamper   A hand held plastic device that fits inside the coffee basket to compress the ground espresso into a level bed and provide resistance by restricting the flow of water through the espresso grind.

Even under pressure, water will follow the path of least resistance, and a level bed of compressed espresso in the coffee basket will help insure an even saturation of the espresso grind. The tamper should have a flat surface and is often two-sided; one side fits in the one-cup coffee basket and the other side is slightly larger to fit inside the two-cup coffee basket.

Some espresso machines feature a built-in tamper. The tamp can be critical; it can correct a grind that is too coarse, but it can also create a complete block in the brew head if the grind is too fine. A slight twist to the tamp will polish off the level of espresso grind and result in a perfect espresso with crema.

temperature Pump-driven espresso machines (and piston lever systems) control temperatures thermostatically to keep the brewing temperature below boiling (from 192°F to 197°F) and the temperature for generating steam above boiling (from 250°F to 270°F). Because espresso is brewed in individual servings, in order to retain heat, the brew head, filter holder and espresso cup should be pre-heated. Steamed milk should not reach the scalding temperature of 150°F or the froth will dissipate and the milk will have a burnt taste.

thermal block A radiator-like device with a heating element in thin coiled channels that flash-heat water. The thermal block replaces the boiler in home espresso machines. The separate brewing and steaming temperatures in the thermal block are controlled thermostatically.

Water is pumped from the reservoir and pulsed into the thermal block where it is flash heated for brewing espresso (under boiling) or generating steam (above boiling). Steam is continuous in a thermal block system, as long as there is water in the reservoir from which the pump can draw. The use of filtered or bottled water is highly recommended with a thermal block machine to avoid the build-up of calcium deposits in the thermal block channels.

thermometer Commercial Baristas
will often use a thermometer clipped
inside the frothing pitcher to gauge the
temperature of the milk in the steaming
or frothing process. Milk scalds at
temperatures over 150°F, and experts claim the
milk temperature should range from 135°F to 150°F. Scalding
milk when frothing will dissipate the froth and impart a burnt taste
to steamed milk that ruins the flavor of milk-based espresso drinks.

thermostat(s) An electrical device designed to maintain the water
temperature at precise brewing and steaming levels. Espresso
machine thermostats are rated in either Fahrenheit or Centigrade.
Electric non-pump espresso machines have one thermostat that
maintains the temperature above 200°F.

There are two thermostats in a pump-driven espresso machine:
one to control the brewing temperature below 198°F and the
second to control the steaming temperature above 250°F. Some
machines have three thermostats; the third is a safety cut-off that
shuts down the machine in the event any of the components
overheat beyond the thermostatic setting.

tryer A wooden scoop used in the roasting process to check the
color of the beans in the roaster. Each varietal reacts differently to
the high heat of the roasting oven, and the roastmaster relies on
sight, sound and smell to gauge the degree of roast.

Turkish coffee A very finely ground powder-like coffee
boiled with water repeatedly in a
small pot called an ibrik. Turkish
coffee is served in small demi-tasse
cups, and the grounds are consumed
with the coffee, usually heavily
sweetened with sugar and
cardamom.

Because of the gritty consistency, Turkish coffee is an acquired taste still popular in the Middle East, North Africa and Southeastern Europe.

underextraction The use of a grind that is not tamped properly, too coarse, or not fresh, will allow water to pass through the coffee quickly and not saturate the grind to extract the true espresso flavor. An underextracted espresso is watery, weak and without crema.

vanilla A flavoring extract from the bean pods of tropical tall climbing orchids. Vanillin is a colorless crystalline compound extracted from vanilla beans, also made synthetically. Vanilla in syrup or powder form is a popular flavoring for cappuccino, lattes and steamers.

varietal Straight coffees in the green bean stage are called varietals, and the delicate roasting process brings out the subtle characteristics of each varietal. Blending mixes two or more straight coffees (varietals) after roasting.

ventilating Flushing or running fresh water through the espresso system to prime the pump with fresh water, pre-heat the brew head and filter holder, and eliminate air pockets that may have formed in the system. See Priming.

warranty Espresso machine manufacturers/importers offer a limited warranty against defects in material and workmanship of their equipment. The time period is usually one year from date of purchase.

The warranty is limited against what is referred to as "customer abuse" not covered by the warranty. Customer abuse can mean allowing the reservoir to run dry and damage the pump, or dropping the machine and breaking the housing.

The manufacturer/importer has the option of repairing or replacing a unit with defined defects in material or workmanship within the specified warranty period. Refer to the instruction manual and warranty card for specifics related to the warranty of your particular machine. Out-of-warranty service is available at the owner's expense after the specified warranty period.

water An espresso serving is 98% water, and the quality of water used will directly affect the flavor of any brewed coffee, especially espresso. If the water is heavily chlorinated or very hard, you may wish to consider using filtered or bottled water (not distilled water).

The use of bottled water also prevents the harmful build-up of calcium deposits in the system. Over a period of time, a build-up of calcium will reduce the power of the machine and can cause damage. Espresso machines should be decalcified periodically, depending on the type of water and how often the machine is used. Distilled water is not recommended because it is flat and flavorless.

water reservoir The vessel that holds fresh water drawn into the espresso system by the pump. Water reservoir capacities vary from 24 ounces to 98 ounces and up to 1 gallon. The capacity of the reservoir can be an important factor when entertaining, and the water reservoir on most machines can be refilled while the machine is operating.

The water reservoir should never be allowed to run dry, since the siphon hose will then draw air into the pump, which can cause damage. Do not confuse the water reservoir with the boiler in a pump-boiler system. Even though there may be water in the reservoir, the boiler may be empty and should be refilled by priming the system.

Some water reservoirs use a gravity feed system, some have a built-in siphon hose, and others have one or two siphon hoses that drop into the water supply.

water softener Used to condition or soften the water through a plastic cylinder that is fitted in the water reservoir to reduce the build-up of calcium in the system. The cylinder is either replaced with a new cartridge or can be regenerated periodically with salt, similar to a home water softening system. In areas with very hard water, the water softener can be a useful feature, but the use of bottled water is always recommended to improve the coffee flavor.

wattage Home espresso machine wattage reflects the electrical consumption required to operate the machine. The wattage consumed by home espresso machines varies from 750 to 1500 watts. It is important that the electrical circuit used to operate the machine is not overloaded with other appliances for optimum performance from the espresso machine.

The heating element and pump are two factors that contribute to total machine wattage consumption. A larger heating element in the boiler or thermal block will use more electricity, and the wattage of the pump (50 to 70 watts) also affects the total wattage of the machine. Grinders consume from 100 to 150 watts.

Yemen   A kingdom of the Southwest Arabian peninsula, Yemen joined the United Arab States in 1958. Supposedly, the Coffea arabica coffee species traveled across the Red Sea to Yemen during the Ethiopian invasion of Southern Arabia in 515 A.D.

Zaire   Formerly the Belgian Congo region of Africa, the Coffea robusta (canephora) species of coffee was first discovered growing wild in Zaire. Robusta beans are cultivated at lower altitudes for the hardiness and fertility of the tree, generally used for commercial (high volume) or soluble (instant) coffees. Some roasters include robusta in their espresso blends due to the high fat content that they believe increases the crema.

zester   A handheld gadget that cuts the rind of citrus fruits in spirals for garnishing espresso-related beverages, such as espresso romano served with a lemon peel.

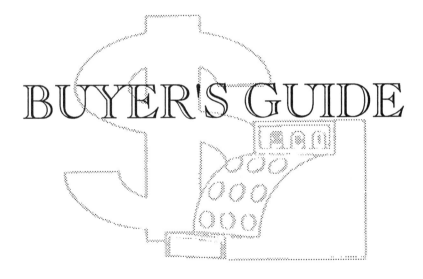

BUYER'S GUIDE

BUYER'S GUIDE TO ESPRESSO MACHINES

The following guidelines are intended to assist you in matching machine features to your personal needs. Before investing in a top of the line machine, you should ask yourself several questions:

1. Will you prepare more "straight" espresso or mostly milk-based drinks, such as cappuccino and lattes?

2. How often will the machine be in actual use - daily, twice a week, weekends, or just on holidays and for entertaining?

3. Do you have space available to keep the espresso machine on the kitchen counter? If so, are you sure the machine is not too tall for the distance between your kitchen counter and cabinets?

4. Are you willing to maintain your machine for optimum performance, including frequent priming, pre-heating and cleaning the machine? Or are you looking for a hassle-free Sunday morning latte?

For preparing mostly milk-based espresso beverages with a limited budget, either a Moka stove-top with stove-top steamer or electric non-pump machine would be good introductory equipment. As you become accustomed to the brewing and steaming processes, while investigating more sophisticated machines on the market, you may decide to spend a year-end bonus or add an upgraded machine to your wish-list.

The preference for straight espresso at home on a regular basis would, however, indicate the need for a more expensive pump-driven or piston lever machine in order to extract a true espresso with crema. In general, a more expensive unit tends to feature a sturdier construction and provide greater pressure in the brewing and steaming modes. A less expensive version of the same type of machine may feature a plastic machine housing, as opposed to metal.

Rely on your specialty retailer to demonstrate equipment in-store, and feel free to ask questions when shopping for espresso equipment. Reputable retailers take pride in their business and will welcome your interest in their products.

Storing your espresso equipment on a kitchen counter is more convenient and inspires frequent use. A taller piston lever machine or pump-driven unit on a base may be too tall to fit conveniently between the kitchen counter and cabinets. If you are considering the purchase of larger equipment, measure the space available so that you can admire the workmanship and will not need to store your machine in a lower cabinet when not in use.

Even purchasing the most expensive machine in the world will not insure an espresso with crema or frothy cappuccino, unless you keep your machine clean. This includes priming frequently through the brew head and steam pipe, keeping the shower disk free of coffee residue, and periodically decalcifying the machine, or using bottled or filtered water to avoid calcium deposits.

Cost is not the only consideration in shopping for espresso equpiment. Evaluate the performance you will expect from your machine, how often you will use it, where you will store it, and if you will maintain the machine for optimum performance and maximum enjoyment.

FEATURES TO LOOK FOR
WHEN PURCHASING ESPRESSO
EQUIPMENT

Consider how often the machine will be in use and determine the power of the equipment you will need. Your specialty coffee retailer can provide valuable information and in-store demonstration prior to your purchase.

Pump:
The pump is vital to provide the necessary pressure to quickly force water through a fine espresso grind and extract the true espresso flavor with crema. Or, consider a piston lever system where pulling down on the lever lowers a piston that creates pressure instead of a pump.

Construction:
A quality machine will be well designed and sturdy. The metal parts should be plated and smooth. The electrical switches should be of high quality. The machine housing should be easy to clean.

Operation:
The controls should be easy to understand and operate. The machine should have status or ready lights to indicate when the

proper temperature has been reached for either brewing espresso or generating steam. A power On/Off light is an important safety feature.

Filter Holder:
The filter holder should be heavy, such as chrome-plated brass, since the retention of heat is important for making café-quality espresso.

Water Reservoir:
The water reservoir should be easy to fill and empty, and made of rigid, sturdy plastic. The water level should be visible, since operating the machine with an empty water reservoir can damage the pump.

Steam Pipe:
The steam vent pipe should be adjustable (swivel) and be long enough to reach into a pitcher for frothing.

Investigate features, such as special filter holders that restrict the flow of water to build additional pressure in the delivery group, or a built-in tamper. The machine should have at least two thermostats and a third cut-off thermostat is an important safety feature. And make sure the Owner's Manual and warranty card are included with your machine.

BUYER'S GUIDE TO BURR GRINDERS

The purchase of a burr grinder to accompany a pump-driven or piston lever machine will, eventually, prove to be a good return on investment. Whole beans retain their freshness longer than pre-ground coffee, and grinding espresso to a consistent, fine grind just before brewing helps ensure the formation of crema.

The fineness of the grind for your machine will depend on the pressure developed in the brewing mode. A more powerful machine will accept a finer grind, and a burr grinder with adjustable indexes controls the consistency of the grind.

There are currently many more home espresso machines to choose from than burr grinders, but, as the popularity of espresso increases, more burr grinders will become available. Lesser expensive burr grinders tend to have a smaller bean hopper capacity and a smaller set of burrs with fewer indexes. Larger and more expensive burr grinders have a deeper taper to the burrs to maintain the consistency of the grind and more precise indexes to adjust the grind.

Some burr grinders feature an interchangeable collection chamber and espresso doser, and others have either a permanent collection chamber or a permanent espresso doser. Because it takes a good amount of coffee to fill the dosing mechanism, using an espresso doser to grind in small quantities tends to waste coffee. Ground espresso exposed to oxygen will lose its flavor in several hours. Unless you grind a fair amount of espresso on a regular basis, you may not need a permanent espresso doser.

Whole beans should not be stored in the bean hopper. Only the amount of beans that will be ground at one time should be poured into the bean hopper.

In the long run, a burr grinder should pay for itself because whole beans retain their freshness longer than pre-ground.

GIFT-GIVING IDEAS

As espresso and cappuccino increase in popularity, espresso equipment can be a welcome holiday, executive or bridal gift. Remember to consider the recipient, and ask the same shopping questions - how often will the machine be used; will they prepare more espresso than milk-based drinks; where will the machine be stored; and will the recipient maintain their new machine? Espresso equipment and accessories are a great gift idea to meet almost any budget.

If you know someone already owns and enjoys their espresso machine, consider a compliment to their favorite appliance. Components to consider are:

A grinder: blade grinder for stove-top, electric non-pump, or drip coffee makers; or a burr grinder for the owner of a piston lever or pump-driven espresso machine

An attractive storage container with a special blend of whole beans or pre-ground espresso roast compatible to their machine

Cappuccino toppings (chocolate, cinnamon and vanilla) and latte flavorings (syrups) to complete any home espresso bar

Decorated demi-tasse, cappuccino or latte cups and saucers to compliment their dinnerware or kitchen decor

Create your own "Crema Kit" with a gift basket of assorted accessories, such as a grounds tray, tamper, steaming pitcher, demi-spoons, frothing thermometer, grinder brush, toppings and flavorings, espresso pods, or a new blend of espresso roast you want them to try.

ESPRESSO EQUIPMENT RECORD

Espresso Machine Brand Name: _____

Model/Serial No.: _____

Date Purchased: _____

Purchased From: _____

_____

_____

Purchase Price: _____

Warranty Information: _____

Manufacturer Name: _____

Address: _____

_____

Grinder Brand Name: _____

Model/Serial No.: _____

Date Purchased: _____

Purchased From: _____

_____

_____

Purchase Price: _____

Warranty Information: _____

Manufacturer Name: _____

Address: _____

Service History: _____

_____

_____

_____

ABOUT THE AUTHORS

Bernard N. Mariano

An importer of fashion housewares products since 1949, Bernie Mariano was one of the first to introduce many well-known brands to the U.S. market including; Le Creuset cookware; Pillivuyt porcelain; Sabatier knives; and Melior, Bialetti, Rotel and Rancilio coffee equipment.

In association with Willard G. Asmus, Bernie pioneered the gourmet shop concept in the 1950's. As president of Schiller & Asmus/Le Creuset of America, in 1974 he developed one of the first coordinated coffee, tea and espresso merchandising programs for specialty retailers nationwide. Bernie's first book was "The Gourmet Product Retailer - Challenge of the '80's" published in 1981.

Although Bernie has received many awards, the most notable is L'Ordre National du Mérite with the rank of knighthood, presented to him in 1978 by Valery Giscard d'Estaing for his contributions to the liberation of France as a member of General Patton's Third Army during WWII, and for his contributions to improving trade relations between the United States and France.

Bernie is a leading authority on espresso equipment for home use. Having written dozens of instruction manuals for espresso machine manufacturers, he realized the need for a consumer guide to broaden the enjoyment of café-quality espresso and cappuccino at home in America. Bernie is the author of the 44-page espresso guide "In Search of the Espresso Secret - Crema" published by Trendex International in 1991.

Jill West

A 16-year veteran of the housewares industry, Jill West holds a Bachelor of Arts degree from Lawrence University, Appleton, Wisconsin. As a language major, Jill studied in France and Germany and participated in business training programs in Europe.

While working for a Chicago law firm, Jill was recruited by Schiller & Asmus/Le Creuset of America, a national distributor of imported housewares, as the bilingual assistant to the president and CEO, Bernie Mariano. One of Jill's responsibilities was maintaining trade relations with foreign manufacturers. In the 1980's her expertise became freight forwarding, importing product from Canada, France, Germany, Italy, Switzerland and the Far East, and exporting American-made product to France and Japan.

Trendex International, Inc.

Bernie Mariano and Jill West co-founded Trendex International in 1983 as consultants to foreign manufacturers of upscale housewares products interested in penetrating the American market. Recognizing the growth potential of the espresso phenomenon in the United States, Trendex developed a national marketing program in 1987 to import a variety of home espresso machines and a selection of espresso accessories.

The "Espresso Encyclopedia" is the second book published by Trendex International dedicated to the American consumer in search of the ultimate espresso experience.

The

Espresso Quarterly

Newsletter

Free Subscription Offer

The new Espresso Quarterly will keep you informed about the latest trends in the specialty coffee industry, new product introductions, with hints and tips from roasters and retailers.

If you would like to be added to our mailing list, please clip and mail us the following page. The first issue of The Espresso Quarterly will be published April 1, 1995.

Completing the short questionnaire will help us include your areas of interest in The Espresso Quarterly newsletter. Thank you!

To receive your free subscription, please mail the facing page to:

Trendex International, Inc.
Department B
1540 Merchandise Mart
Chicago, IL 60654

Espresso Quarterly Subscription Form

Yes, please send The Espresso Quarterly free of charge to:

Name: _____

Address: _____

City/State/Zip: _____

Completing the following questionnaire will help us include your areas of interest in future issues of The Espresso Quarterly. Thank you!

Do you own an espresso machine? ___ Yes ___ No

If so, what type of machine: Stove-Top _____
                               Electric Non-Pump _____
                               Piston Lever _____
                               Pump-Boiler _____
                               Thermal Block _____

What is the brand name of your machine:
_____ Model No. _____

Do you recall the price you paid for your machine? $_____

Did you receive your machine as a gift? ___ Yes ___ No

How long have you owned your machine?
___ 1-3 years ___ 4-6 years ___ 7-10+ years

How often do you use your machine?
___ Daily ___ Weekly ___ Twice Weekly ___ Rarely

Quick Reference Index